I0759484

A LITTLE ME TIME WITH GOD

365 Daily Devotions

BroadStreet
PUBLISHING

BroadStreet Publishing Group, LLC.
Savage, Minnesota, USA
Broadstreetpublishing.com

A LITTLE ME TIME WITH GOD

9781424570911
9781424570928 (eBook)

Typesetting and design by Garborg Design Works | garborgdesign.com
Editorial services by Michelle Winger | literallyprecise.com.
Compiled by Natasha Marcellus.

Printed in China.

25 26 27 28 29 30 31 7 6 5 4 3 2 1

"Come with me by yourselves to a quiet place and get some rest."

Mark 6:31 NIV

INTRODUCTION

In the busyness of life, *A Little Me Time with God* offers you a daily invitation to pause, breathe, and reconnect with the one who knows you best. Discover a deeper sense of identity, rest, courage, and peace.

Each page is designed to bring you into a moment of stillness where you can hear God's gentle whispers and find renewed strength for the day. Devotional entries, Scriptures, and prayers help remind you that you are valued, loved, and equipped to face life's challenges—not alone, but with God by your side.

Embrace the daily practice of slipping away for rest and renewal and watch as your relationship with God deepens, bringing fresh purpose and restored joy.

JANUARY

"Seek first the kingdom of God and his righteousness, and all these things will be provided for you."

MATTHEW 6:33 CSB

LENS OF MERCY

You are near, Lord,
and all your commands are true.
Long ago I learned from your decrees
that you have established them forever.

Psalm 119:151-152 CSB

Fix your thoughts on the nearness of God today. Make it a priority to bring your attention back to his presence throughout your day. As you do, reflect on the fruit of his presence in your life. Where is there love, joy, peace, kindness, and graciousness? Where is there room to both rest and grow in who you are?

The commands of the Lord are not meant to burden you. As you read the Word, you can find encouragement, direction, acceptance, and encouragement. Each part is woven together by the unending love of God. Read it through the lens of mercy and turn your attention to his faithfulness.

Faithful One, I lean on your faithfulness today. As I bring my attention and focus back to your presence, release your peace, wisdom, and truth into my heart.

HE SINGS OVER YOU

The LORD your God is in your midst,
a mighty one who will save;
he will rejoice over you with gladness;
he will quiet you by his love;
he will exult over you with loud singing.

ZEPHANIAH 3:17 ESV

God doesn't want you to miss out on the freedom of his love. He delights over you with gladness, and he rejoices over you with singing. He longs for you to see yourself and others through his perspective. His love for you does not come from obligation but from a pure and simple desire to be close to you.

God's heart is tender toward you. Don't resist the graciousness of his affection. If you focus on the parts of you that seem inadequate, you'll miss the contentedness that is found in his presence. Your kind Father delights in you. He doesn't expect you to present your best self or clean up your mistakes before you get close to him.

Lord God, there is no one like you. Your love is pure, true, and life changing. Keep my heart soft and remind me of how you see me.

BEYOND BASIC

"The Father himself loves you."

JOHN 16:27 NIV

If you were to spend every day of your life meditating on the truth that Jesus revealed in this verse, you would never reach the end of its impact. Love is the basis of the kingdom of God. It is who God is. Experiencing his love for you and sharing it with others is worthy of your entire life.

Instead of letting the idea of God's love become trite, press in to know him in a deeper way. There is richness that can only be found through a dedicated and intentional pursuit of the Lord. His love is not a basic principle of the gospel that you move on from; it's the epitome of who he is, and he longs for you to understand how he feels about you.

Good Father, I admit that I need a fresh revelation of your love today. As I focus on your love, reveal what I could not perceive before. I want to know your heart in a deeper way.

LOOK UP

Raise your eyes on high
And see who has created these stars,
The One who brings out their multitude by number,
He calls them all by name.

Isaiah 40:26 NASB

When life is overwhelming, it can feel as if the walls of this world are closing in on you. This is the perfect time to expand your perspective and allow God to lift your spirit. As you turn your attention to him, he will remind you of his attentive care and faithful sovereignty. Even your greatest trials do not overwhelm him.

Today, put yourself in a position to marvel at God's greatness in comparison to your smallness. Knowing that God is much larger than you can imagine brings comfort and a sense of security. Whether you stare over an expansive body of water, stand under the vast sky, or climb a mountain to gain a higher perspective, take some time to physically get into a space that reminds you of the Creator and his vast power.

Creator, thank you for the perspective creation brings. Help me find rest, peace, and comfort in your presence.

STEADY AND STRONG

The Sovereign LORD is my strength!
He makes me as surefooted as a deer,
able to tread upon the heights.

HABAKKUK 3:19 NLT

When you are overtired and worn-down, it can be difficult to focus on anything else. Yet, the Scriptures say over and over again that the Lord is your strength. In your weakness, he makes you strong. When you run out of your own vigor, lean on him and let him steady your feet.

God sees every challenge you face. He knows exactly what you need to get through each day. His eyes are on you, and he is eager to guide you through whatever life throws at you. You are valued, loved, and fully equipped because God has deemed it so. He is the reason you are strong, and he is the one who has faithfully provided for you. If you look to him, he will not let you down.

Lord, make my feet sure and my resolve strong. When I have nothing more of my own to give, you always have an abundance of what I need. Fill me afresh today.

HE SEES

"The LORD—the LORD is a compassionate and gracious God, slow to anger and abounding in faithful love and truth."

EXODUS 34:6 CSB

God sees what you cannot. He is aware of the full picture of your life as well as the intentions and desires of your heart. He knows everything, yet he is kind, merciful and abounding in faithfulness. He does not turn you away when you are weak, and he does not chastise you for your mistakes.

When you feel yourself jumping to conclusions about how God might react to you, bring your thoughts under the canopy of his grace. Remind yourself of the strength of his character and the reliability of his kindness. May you find yourself enveloped in his mercy today, and from that place give out the abundance of his pure love to others.

Gracious God, you see my heart fully. Have mercy on me and wrap me in your arms. When my perspective is wrong, draw me back to the truth.

CONFIDENT IN HIM

With God's power working in us, God can do much, much more than anything we can ask or imagine.

EPHESIANS 3:20 NCV

There is value in hard work and focus. Even so, there are limits to your abilities, and you cannot account for unforeseen obstacles in life. You cannot control the actions of others, accidents that will happen, or how loss will affect you. When your plans go off-track, don't lose hope. God is faithful, and his mercy will hold you together.

God is able to do immeasurably more than anything you can imagine or ask him to do. Let yourself be empowered by his ability more than you are confident in your own. He is the only one who can resurrect the dead and redeem what is lost. Spend time in his presence and allow his strength to fill you with hopeful confidence. He will not let you down.

Mighty God, I know that you are able to do more than I can even venture to imagine. Strengthen my faith and empower me to honor you with everything I have. I trust you to lead me.

PRACTICE GRATITUDE

Oh, give thanks to the LORD!
Call upon His name;
Make known His deeds among the peoples!

1 CHRONICLES 16:8 NKJV

Practicing gratitude is like giving yourself a beautiful gift. The habit of acknowledging what you are thankful for creates space in your life for contentment, peace, and confidence. The more you direct your attention to the good things God has given you, the less distracted you will be by the constantly shifting standards of the world.

You don't have to ignore your needs or frustrations in order to be thankful. Gratitude can seamlessly co-exist with grief, heartache, and frustration. You can bring those things to God, expecting him to handle them while you focus on the good gifts he has given you. As you go about your day, make note of the things that offer peace, joy, hope, and love.

Lord, thank you for this day and the opportunity to experience more of your goodness. Give me grace to bring my burdens to you. I trust you to handle the things I can't.

LOOK FORWARD

I don't depend on my own strength to accomplish this; however I do have one compelling focus: I forget all of the past as I fasten my heart to the future instead.

PHILIPPIANS 3:13 TPT

Ruminating on the past can make you feel stuck in the present. When shame comes knocking on the door of your heart, it is important to invite Jesus to show you his perspective. He doesn't hold you accountable to the sins he's already forgiven. There is no need to hold yourself as a prisoner when he has given you freedom.

You were never meant to achieve perfection. Instead of dwelling on the things you can't change, you can shift your focus to who God is, who he says you are, and what he has in store for your future. Learning from the past is one thing, but dwelling on your mistakes to your own detriment isn't helpful. Allow yourself to be grounded in Christ's love and move forward with confidence.

Lord Jesus, give me courage to let go of shame. I choose to follow you even when I am overwhelmed by my circumstances. Thank you for loving me and calling me yours.

FOLLOW THE SPIRIT

Hope does not put us to shame, because God's love has been poured into our hearts through the Holy Spirit who has been given to us.

ROMANS 5:5 ESV

The Holy Spirit does not work within your heart to produce shame but to shower you in love. The Spirit is a gift from God, and his primary intention is to point you toward truth. He was not given to you to babysit you or correct you with a prideful and condescending attitude. His voice is gentle, and his words are life-giving.

When you open yourself up to the leadership of the Spirit, he will renew your hope and remind you of God's love. He will encourage, comfort, and guide you. Condemnation, confusion, and shame do not come from the Holy Spirit. Trust him to hold your heart gently and remind you of God's mercy and grace when you need it most.

Holy Spirit, flood my senses with the power of your love until I am filled with a sense of expansive belonging, empowered determination, and peaceful resolution.

DECLARATION OF TRUTH

He has brought me to his banquet hall,
And his banner over me is love.

Song of Solomon 2:4 NASB

When you live under the banner of God's love, no arrows of accusation can rip you apart. Like a banner provides the intention or purpose of an event or group of people, God's love declares the truth of who you are. His love for you announces to the world that you are accepted, cherished, and valued. His love declares that you are welcome, redeemed, and set free.

When you are tempted to look at yourself through your own eyes, redirect your thoughts to what God says. Allow his love to be the foundation of your self-image. Believing the truth about who you are is just as important as behaving in way that honors God. He longs for you to see yourself through his eyes. His banner over you is love, and he sees you through a lens of mercy and grace.

Merciful God, thank you for the power of your persistent love. Help me adjust my thinking in areas where I am out of alignment. I surrender to your definition of the truth.

GOD'S WILL

Don't copy the behavior and customs of this world, but let God transform you into a new person by changing the way you think. Then you will learn to know God's will for you, which is good and pleasing and perfect.

Romans 12:2 NLT

The way you think dictates the way you act. If you are full of fear, skepticism, and anger, then the path you choose will show it. If you are confident in God's love, sure of his care, and unwavering in trust, your life will bear the fruit of those things.

The only way for your heart to be transformed is to spend time in God's presence. The closer you are to him the more opportunities he has to shower you with love and soften the parts of your heart that are hard or wounded. If you let him, he will faithfully shift the way you think and move. You can trust him with every part of yourself because his will for you is good and pleasing.

Spirit, transform my thoughts in your gracious presence. I don't want my life to reflect the values of the world. I want to reflect you from the inside out.

HIS PERSPECTIVE

You created my inmost being;
you knit me together in my mother's womb.
I praise you because I am fearfully and wonderfully made;
your works are wonderful,
I know that full well.

PSALM 139:13-14 NIV

When you find your worth in what others think of you, it is as if you are trying to hit a moving target. The world's standards and the opinions of other people are constantly changing. In contrast, God's perception of you never changes. He looks at you with loving affection, and he always will.

You don't have to change a single thing to find yourself fully loved and accepted by your Father in heaven. You were created with joy and intention, and every part of you speaks to God's creativity. When you are tempted to cover up your flaws or hide them in shame, remember that your Maker sees you clearly and welcomes you into his presence.

Creator, I want to love myself the way that you love me. Your love makes me feel worthy and noticed.

SET FREE

"Let us praise the LORD, the God of Israel,
because he has come to help his people
and has given them freedom.
He has given us a powerful Savior."

LUKE 1:68-69 NCV

God did not leave you without help in this world. He sent his Son to help you and liberate you. No matter what hard times you go through, you are free from the curse of sin, fear, and death. You are liberated in Christ now and for eternity.

No one can take away the power of love that saves you. Praise God because you have been set free! Turn your attention to the very near presence of God and rejoice in his perfect plan of redemption. Through Christ, he has given you everything you will ever need. Fix your eyes on your Savior and let the beauty of his love transform your heart.

Savior, thank you for the freedom I find in you. Continue to transform my heart as I put my trust in you.

FAITHFUL PROVISION

"Don't strive for what you should eat and what you should drink, and don't be anxious."

LUKE 12:29 CSB

Worrying and striving will deplete your emotional energy. Jesus asks you to lay aside your worries and give up striving for the necessities. He invites you to put your needs into his hands and trust him to provide for you.

Giving your anxiety to God is not a passive solution. When you actively surrender your worries, he takes them from you and gives you peace in exchange. Instead of spending your time ruminating or spiraling into negative thought patterns, direct your energy toward surrendering your burdens. Breathe deep in God's presence and trust with the things you cannot handle alone.

Trustworthy Savior, I don't want to keep toiling for what you offer me for free. Rather than striving for the bare minimum, I trust you to provide.

HE REDEEMS

"The Son of Man has come to seek and to save that which was lost."

LUKE 19:10 NKJV

Jesus is the redeemer of all things that are lost or broken. Through his death and resurrection, he did what no one else could. He provided a way for you to be absolved of your guilt and shame forever. There is nothing in your life that is more powerful than his ability to redeem it.

Don't let shame keep you from exposing your entire heart to Jesus. Every part of your life is welcome at the cross. Surrender your whole self to him no matter how confused, frustrated, overwhelmed, or ashamed you feel. He welcomes you into his presence with mercy and grace. He offers you freedom when you don't deserve it, and he offers you wholeness and new life.

Jesus Christ, my hope is in you. Come into my heart and bring restoration and new life. Thank you for your faithful redemption.

REAL NEEDS

It is through him that you now believe in God, who raised him from the dead and glorified him, so that you would fasten your faith and hope in God alone.

1 Peter 1:21 TPT

Consider today what your hopes are fixed on. Is it the next promotion, an overhaul of your finances, or a relationship that you feel could fix everything? It's normal to think that one or two physical changes would give you exactly what you want. It doesn't take long to realize that once you receive what you had long awaited, you latch onto the next thing.

What you really need is a transformative relationship with Jesus Christ. He offers fulfillment for your deepest needs in his presence. He is the well you draw from, and he alone can satisfy your soul. Even when none of your circumstances look how you want, you can look to the one who dwells within you and offers you peace.

Faithful One, I choose to look to you today for all that I need. I bring you my unfulfilled longings and ask for your presence to fill me up with the wonderful goodness of your love. I fasten my faith to you.

PATH TO MATURITY

When I was a child, I talked like a child, I thought like a child, I reasoned like a child. When I became a man, I put the ways of childhood behind me.

1 Corinthians 13:11 NIV

Growth and maturity don't happen overnight. Your walk with God will be filled with adjustments, repentance, change, and redemption. Just as a child matures into an adult, you will mature in your walk with God. If you let him, the Holy Spirit will steadily guide you along the path toward maturity.

Don't be discouraged if you aren't where you'd like to be. If you are surrendered to God's leadership, you can trust his timing. He knows exactly how to lead you through each challenge you face, and he knows how to cultivate fruit in your life. Take a deep breath and lean into God's presence rather than fretting over perceived progress.

Father, thank you for the chance to change, mature, and grow. I embrace it and I trust you to guide me. Give me the humility needed to embrace growth.

PARTNER WITH HIM

"Be strong and courageous, and do the work. Don't be afraid or discouraged, for the LORD God, my God, is with you. He will not fail you or forsake you. He will see to it that all the work related to the Temple of the LORD is finished."

1 CHRONICLES 28:20 NLT

Having faith in God does not mean sitting back and waiting for him to move on your behalf in every season of life. There is power in your partnership. Be strong and courageous and put your faith in God. Allow him to do his part, and obediently do what he asks of you.

Instead of getting lost in what-ifs today, take hold of what you know to be true. Obedience isn't complicated. God doesn't ask you to do anything without his help. No matter what he calls you to do today, he is with you every step of the way. He is the one who equips you to love your family, do your job, and share his love with everyone around you.

Lord, help me to focus on your help and the work that is mine to do. You are my strength and courage, and I choose to partner with you.

ALWAYS THE SAME

Jesus Christ is the same yesterday and today and forever.

Hebrews 13:8 NASB

In a world full of constant change, there is one who remains the same forever. He is forever moved by compassion, full of marvelous mercy, and overflowing with kindness. He is just, true, and always sees things clearly.

When you feel overwhelmed by the unknowns of tomorrow, you can take refuge in God's consistency. He is a safe place to find shelter. He sees the end from the beginning and everything between. He is full of wisdom, and he can restore even what feels irredeemable. Throw the anchor of your hope into the abundant waters of his strong love, for they will never run dry.

Unchanging One, as I meditate on your goodness and your grandeur, I cannot help but be filled with the peace of your presence. You are trustworthy and true, and you will never change.

LAW OF LOVE

"Render true judgments, show kindness and mercy to one another, do not oppress the widow, the fatherless, the sojourner, or the poor, and let none of you devise evil against another in your heart."

ZECHARIAH 7:8-10 ESV

Love is liberating, not controlling. It is full of kindness and grace. It is not biased, nor is it manipulative. The law of love reigns over every tradition, regulation, and law of this world. You are no longer bound by a list of rules and standards you can't meet. Instead, you have been set free by Christ's love.

God's love for you is extravagant and kind. This is how you are meant to treat others as well. Love should be the foundation for everything you do. This is only possible when you recognize Jesus as your life source. Your ability to love others comes directly from spending time with God and receiving his love for you.

Lord, when I consider how you instruct us to live and how I actually treat others, I see so much room for growth in myself. May I follow your path of love, even and especially when it feels hard to do so.

HE INVITES YOU

"See! I stand at the door and knock. If anyone hears my voice and opens the door, I will come in to him and eat with him, and he with me."

REVELATION 3:20 CSB

Jesus stands at the door of your heart, knocking. Do you hear his voice? Open the door to him and welcome him in. There is unbroken fellowship in his presence, and you will find abundantly more than you need. He is good, and his love transforms you as often as you will let it.

You can remain closed off to the ways of Christ, or you can embrace what he offers you. It all starts in your heart. As you surrender to his love, he will faithfully meet you with mercy and grace. If you pursue him, he will not hide from you. If you seek him, he will not turn you away. Run to him with confidence, knowing that he wants to be with you.

Jesus Christ, I don't want to struggle on my own any longer. Even when I feel resistance, I will open the door to you. I want to be washed in the refreshing waters of your love and restored in your mercy.

AUDIENCE OF ONE

"Pray to your Father, who cannot be seen. Your Father can see what is done in secret, and he will reward you."

MATTHEW 6:6 NCV

The good things you do won't always be visible. There might be areas of your life where you feel underappreciated or overlooked. When this happens, remember that God is always aware of you. He sees every single act of service, and he accounts for each sacrifice you make. He promises to reward you for your good works, and you can trust that his rewards are far better than the praise or affirmation of other people.

When you feel ignored, run to the secret place with God. Allow him to encourage you. As you trust him with your feelings, he will expand your ability to walk in humility and confidence. With God's approval, you can lay your life down with your head held high.

Father, I know that you see what others miss. I don't want to strive for attention or affirmation from others. Your opinion matters so much more than anyone else's.

NEW SPROUTS

There is hope for a tree, if it is cut down,
That it will sprout again,
And that its tender shoots will not cease.

Job 14:7 NKJV

When you go through hard times, God is still faithful. There is always hope. There is redemption, restoration, and mercy as long as you are living. Even if a tree is cut down, there is hope for it to sprout again. The same is true about your own life.

No matter what setbacks you face, you can trust that there is hope for redemption. New life can sprout from the most desolate situations. In the aftermath of grief, God can restore what is broken and give you hope for the future. He can cultivate fruit in your life even when you don't understand how. Trust him with the parts of your life that feel hopeless or broken.

Restorer, I trust that you are not finished with me yet. Have your way in my life and bring new life out of the ashes. Thank you for never giving up on me.

RECEIVE HIS GIFTS

God will never give you the spirit of fear, but the Holy Spirit who gives you mighty power, love, and self-control.

2 Timothy 1:7 TPT

Though many systems and people of this world lead with fear, God does not. He does not seek to control you through fear, nor does he hold you captive by it. He liberates you with love every single time. Where there is fear in your life, it is certainly not the work of God.

Find refuge in God's presence and allow him to strengthen you. Actively give him your fears and trust that he can handle them. You get to choose how fear impacts your life. You can hold it close, cultivate it, and watch it grow, or you can place it in God's hands and accept his gifts instead. He offers you peace, power, love, and self-control.

Great God, I will not fear what others may say or do against me. I choose to live in the liberation of your love and follow the wisdom of your truth. Your ways are so much better than the ways of this world.

TRUST HIM

Nothing in all creation is hidden from God's sight. Everything is uncovered and laid bare before the eyes of him to whom we must give account.

HEBREWS 4:13 NIV

Nothing in all creation is hidden from God. He sees every part of your heart and every second of your life. He knows your secret fears, and he is aware of your true motivations. This is not meant to cause you shame or embarrassment. Instead, be empowered by the sovereignty of God.

There is security to be found in God's endless knowledge. If he knows everything about you, then he knows exactly how to take care of you and exactly what you need. His sovereignty means that you can give him control and trust that everything he does is founded in mercy and grace. Surrender your whole heart to him and humbly remember that even though he sees all of you, his love for you is extravagant.

Wise God, I trust that you see what no one else can. Thank you for the security of your love. Help me to trust in your sovereignty and provision.

SEASONS CHANGE

Rejoice, you people of Jerusalem!
Rejoice in the LORD your God!
For the rain he sends demonstrates his faithfulness.
Once more the autumn rains will come,
as well as the rains of spring.

JOEL 2:23 NLT

If you find yourself longing for winter's end, know that it is coming. The sun rises each morning, bringing with it fresh mercy. There is nothing on earth that will last forever. The seasons shift and change, and so will your life.

If you are walking through a difficult season, take heart. Remember that change will come, and God will see you through. If you let him, he will guide you and comfort you throughout your journey. Even when the days feel long and things don't move as quickly as you'd like, God is faithful. Rest in the hope that he offers you. The best is still yet to come.

Faithful One, thank you for the promise of your loyal love meeting me with each new sunrise and every turning of the seasons. I trust you, and I look to you for help and hope.

DWELL ON TRUTH

"I am with you always, to the end of the age."

MATTHEW 28:20 NASB

The same promise that Christ gave to his disciples before he ascended to the Father's side is the promise you have to hold onto today. You are never without the presence of God through his Spirit. When you yield your life to Christ, he makes his home in your heart.

You cannot escape the goodness of God. He goes before you to pave the way, and he dwells within you. His mercy is ever-present, and his wisdom is at hand. He is trustworthy and faithful, and you can depend on him every moment of the day. No matter how alone you might feel, determine in your heart to dwell on the truth. God is always with you.

Lord, your presence brings peace, clarity, hope, and joy. I look to you today and put my hope in your present help. Remind me of your nearness when I am discouraged.

EQUIPPED TO UNDERSTAND

Then he opened their minds to understand the Scriptures.

LUKE 24:45 ESV

Scripture is a gift and a blessing. You will find encouragement, hope, correction, and wisdom within the pages of the Word. Don't be intimidated by the Bible's length or language. God is eager and able to give you clarity when you need it. He will open your mind and give you understanding.

Allow the Holy Spirit to guide you as you read Scripture. Lean on him for clarity and trust him to point out the truth you need to hear. As he stirs your heart, press in and allow truth to grow deep roots in your heart. Don't shy away from the parts of the Word that seem difficult. You have everything you need to soak them in and glean from them.

Wise God, I believe that all problems find a solution in you. I come to you for wisdom, strategy, and help. Open my understanding and reveal your ways in practical steps as I spend time in your Word.

DIVINE EXCHANGE

"I will give them a crown to replace their ashes,
and the oil of gladness to replace their sorrow,
and clothes of praise to replace their spirit of sadness."

ISAIAH 61:3 NCV

Though you cannot escape loss in this life, you can trust the one who offers you hope in the midst of it. Trusting God does not mean life becomes pain-free or easy. However, it does mean that you can lean on the one who never grows weary. He has everything you need, and he is generous to share it.

Are there parts of your life that have been reduced to ashes? Have you experienced sorrow too deep to navigate? Is there sadness in your heart that you can't seem to overcome? You are not alone as you walk through these things. God promises you redemption. He is familiar with your pain, and he will not abandon you to it. Rest in the beauty of his presence and receive the strength and peace he offers.

God, thank you for the promise of restoration and redemption. You don't leave me to waste away in the ashes of despair. You lift me up, bind up my wounds, and heal me. Thank you.

SECRETS REVEALED

"He reveals deep and secret things;
He knows what is in the darkness,
And light dwells with Him."

DANIEL 2:22 NKJV

When you give your life to God, he offers you more of himself. As you walk in his ways and seek to love as he does, he gives you the gift of his fellowship. He will meet you with abundant love every time you turn to him.

Taking the time to get to know God is the only way to understand his heart. There aren't shortcuts, and no one can do it for you. As you spend time in his presence, he will share his perspective and teach you about his character. If you seek him, he will reveal his truth, light, and wisdom.

God, I want to know the deep and secret things of your heart. I want to know you more than anything else. You are so worthy of my attention, time, and trust.

FEBRUARY

"Stop fighting, and know that I am God,
exalted among the nations,
exalted on the earth."

Psalm 46:10 CSB

NEW CREATION

If anyone is in Christ, he is a new creation: the old has passed away, and see, the new has come!

2 Corinthians 5:17 CSB

The mistakes of your past have no power over you if you are in Christ. He has made you completely new in his mercy. He does not hold your sins against you, nor are you defined by what others say. You have been liberated from the grip of sin and death.

Christ's mercy is new every day. Anytime you long for a fresh start it is yours. As you surrender at the cross and declare God's lordship over your life, you are transformed into someone new. Though you can't escape the natural consequences of your sin, you can escape eternal accountability for them. God longs for you to experience the freedom he so graciously offers you.

Jesus Christ, thank you for making me a new creation. Thank you for breaking the cycles of sin, shame, and fear. I stand upon the solid rock of your love.

FAITHFUL FOREVER

The Lord Yahweh is always faithful to place you on a firm foundation and guard you from the Evil One.

2 Thessalonians 3:3 TPT

When you trust in the Lord as your Savior, you can be assured that he will always place you on a firm foundation in times of trouble. Even when the winds of trouble blow, you can rest in the safety of his love. He will guard you from the enemy, and he will be with you every step of the way.

Instead of letting anxiety rise as trouble mounts, look to the Lord Yahweh who is always near. Remember that he places your feet on a firm foundation. When you turn to him, he gives you everything you need. He holds you close and shields you from harm.

Faithful Lord, thank you for offering yourself as my hiding place. I run into your presence to find the peace my soul needs. Place me on a firm foundation and guard me from the threats that surround.

INSIDE OUT

"Remain in me, as I also remain in you. No branch can bear fruit by itself; it must remain in the vine. Neither can you bear fruit unless you remain in me."

JOHN 15:4 NIV

Jesus is your connection to the Father. As you abide in him, he nourishes you from the inside out. You cannot bear the fruit of his kingdom apart from him. He is the very source of life, and the author of everything good.

Stay connected to God today. Lean on him instead of trying to push through in your own strength. Deliberately set your thoughts on him and open your heart to him. Let him empower you and give you what you need to live, breathe, and move. Be nourished by the peace of his presence.

Christ, thank you for the power of your grace and mercy in my life. I yield to your presence today. Fill me with peace, joy, hope, and love. Thank you.

SMALL AND SIGNIFICANT

"Do not despise these small beginnings, for the LORD rejoices to see the work begin."

ZECHARIAH 4:10 NLT

Small beginnings are nothing to be ashamed of. In fact, most good things start with seemingly insignificant steps. A tiny seed grows into a flourishing plant, and a fleeting thought transforms into a dream. Each step along the way is important and valuable no matter how small it is.

Instead of being overwhelmed by the unknowns in your life, confidently take each step that God places in front of you. All you need to do is do the next right thing. The more time you spend with God, the more confidence you will have in his voice. As he speaks to you, follow his instructions. He delights in each small step of faith you take.

Lord, thank you that I don't need to see the end from the beginning and every step along the way. You do, and I trust you to guide me with your wisdom, perspective, and truth. You are a reliable leader.

GOOD THOUGHTS

Whatever is true, whatever is honorable, whatever is just, whatever is pure, whatever is lovely, whatever is commendable, if there is any excellence, if there is anything worthy of praise, think about these things.

PHILIPPIANS 4:8 ESV

Your thoughts dictate your actions. Fear, anxiety, temptation, and jealousy are heavy burdens. They inhibit your ability to walk freely and confidently. It's hard to maintain faith when you are overcome by the weight of negative thoughts.

Not every thought is worth your time and attention. It's okay to have a thought and disregard it. This takes discipline and intentionality, but the more you practice the easier it will become. Focus on what God says is good and align your thoughts with his values. Submit your internal commentary to him and allow him to transform the way you think.

Pure One, help me to take my thoughts captive and focus on the things of your kingdom. Align my heart with yours and help me honor you in all I do.

ALONE TIME

"Come away by yourselves to a secluded place and rest a while."

MARK 6:31 NASB

Jesus did not spend all his time with others. He knew the power of rest, and he knew the value of spending quiet time with his Father. He deliberately stepped away from his work in order to be refreshed and restored.

You have not been called to a life of constant work. Sustainable growth happens when there are healthy margins in your life. Take time to rest and find joy. Connect with your Maker and let him revive your soul. Prioritize time to breathe and you will not be disappointed.

Jesus, thank you for the example of prioritizing rest and alone time in your ministry. I don't want to give so much of myself that I lose connection with who I am, who you are, and who you've called me to be.

PATTERNS OF LIFE

"From the beginning I told you
what would happen in the end.
A long time ago I told you things
that have not yet happened.
When I plan something, it happens.
What I want to do, I will do."

ISAIAH 46:10 NCV

Unmet expectations can bring frustration, confusion, and even grief. Sometimes your best efforts and most well laid plans won't work out. While you can't avoid every disappointment, you can place your hope firmly in the God who will never disappoint you. His promises always come to fruition.

God does what he says. Every single plan he makes works out. He is never at a loss, and his plans always prosper. If your soul is anchored to him, you won't be shaken when life feels off-track. Instead of relying on your ability to manage your life, place your confidence in God's promise to make all things right.

Faithful Father, I'm so grateful you aren't surprised by the things that throw me off. Your perspective is perfect, and you are always faithful.

WHAT YOU NEED

If any of you lacks wisdom, he should ask God, who gives to all generously and ungrudgingly, and it will be given to him.

JAMES 1:5 CSB

It is not selfish to ask for what you need. You don't need to try harder or do everything yourself. You were not made to be self-sufficient. God is your Father, and he is not distant. He longs for you to depend on him. You display strength when you readily acknowledge your weaknesses before God.

Do you need wisdom? Ask him for it and he will give it to you in abundance. There's no reason to insist on independence when the God of the entire universe offers you his perspective. The smartest thing you can do is run to his presence at the first sign of trouble. Today, pursue him and allow him to give you what you need.

Wise God, thank you for your wealth of wisdom. Help me run to you as soon as I need help. I trust you go carry me through whatever comes my way.

PRODUCTIVE TRUST

Blessed is the man who trusts in the Lord,
And whose hope is the Lord.
For he shall be like a tree planted by the waters…
And will not fear when heat comes.

Jeremiah 17:7-8 NKJV

Trusting in the Lord does not mean ignoring the realities of your life or the struggles of the world at large. It doesn't mean that you check out of your responsibilities or put on rose colored glasses. Trusting in God is a posture of faith which results in the confidence that God is good no matter what is happening around you.

True trust will yield fruitfulness in your life. As you lean on God, he will give you peace and hope. As you remain connected to him, he will keep you steady despite the challenges you face. He will shield you from anxiety even when the world around you feels chaotic.

Trustworthy One, I choose to put the anchor of my trust in your unchanging character. Move in me, Spirit of God, and produce your fruit in my surrendered life.

THE LIVING EXPRESSION

The Living Expression became a man and lived among us! And we gazed upon his glory, the glory of the One and Only who came from the Father overflowing with tender mercy and truth!

JOHN 1:14 TPT

Jesus is a perfect picture of God. His life perfectly displayed God's character and intentions. If you wonder what God is like, look at Jesus. By studying his life, you can learn exactly how God would operate in any given situation.

Like the people in biblical times, you might assume that God is grandiose, unreachable, and stern. Jesus proved that he is kind, merciful, and compassionate. He longs to be close to you, and his love is extravagant. Today, gaze upon the glory of Christ and let it stir up affection for your good and perfect Father.

Lord Jesus, thank you for breaking down the walls of misunderstanding of who God is. Thank you for teaching me about his kindness and love. Thank you for making a way for me to be with my Father.

CHOOSE YOUR MEASURE

"Give, and it will be given to you. A good measure, pressed down, shaken together and running over, will be poured into your lap. For with the measure you use, it will be measured to you."

Luke 6:38 NIV

One of the main principles of the kingdom of God is generosity. When you give to others, you will receive in the same measure. The benefits of generosity can be internal or external. God may provide physical blessings, but he will definitely provide spiritual ones.

As you give to others, your ability to love expands. You will grow in compassion and experience the fulfillment that comes from laying your life down in a sacrifice of love. It doesn't matter how much you have to give. What matters most is the attitude with which you give and your ability to recognize that the blessings in your life are not yours to hoard.

Generous One, I know I have room to stretch my generosity. Help me to be practical in showing love to others, without needing anything from them in return.

OVERFLOW OF GOODNESS

"A good person produces good things from the treasury of a good heart, and an evil person produces evil things from the treasury of an evil heart. What you say flows from what is in your heart."

LUKE 6:45 NLT

Your life reflects what is going on in your heart. If you have goodness, mercy, and peace in your heart, it will overflow into what you produce with your hands. If you want to live a life that honors God, it all starts with the state of your heart.

As you yield your heart to the Lord, he will transform it. He will lovingly shape and mold your life into something beautiful. He fixes what is broken, and he strengthens you where you are weak. He ministers with kindness and encourages you to stand upon the truth. Today, give him permission to align your heart with his.

Good Father, I want my life to reflect your nature and values. I know that you are loving, patient, kind, and just. Heal my heart and let it reflect your powerful mercy as I live, speak, and interact with others.

FOLLOW HIM

"You shall follow the LORD your God and fear him; and you shall keep His commandments, listen to his voice, serve him, and cling to him."

DEUTERONOMY 13:4 NASB

When you focus your attention on following the Lord, it will affect how you see the world. There is a stark difference between how God operates and how the world operates. God is gracious and merciful, and man-made systems are often harsh and exclusive.

When you find yourself frustrated by how things in this world work, look to the one who does everything well. He is perfect, and he won't let you down. His ways are ideal, and his instructions are worth following. The path he has set for you leads to eternal life and an abundance of blessings. He knows what is best, and he is eager to guide you.

Father, my hope is in you, not in the systems of this world. They will always fail, but your ways never do. I choose to trust you and follow you all the days of my life.

GLORIOUS GRACE

By grace you have been saved through faith, and that not of yourselves; it is the gift of God.

EPHESIANS 2:8 NKJV

God's grace is outrageous. It never runs out, and you can't earn it. There is nothing you can do to become more eligible for grace, and no one can take away the grace you've been given. God offers it to you freely for as long as you live.

You are accepted by God because of Jesus' sacrifice. You are welcome in his presence because of Christ's death and resurrection. The work has already been done. Anything you do to gain God's favor is pointless. Today, lay down your stiving and accept his gift of grace. Open your heart to him and rest in the goodness of the gospel.

Gracious God, I have tasted of your goodness, but I know there is so much more to learn about you. Take me as I am today and give me a fresh revelation of your grace.

PERFECT ONE

"This God, his way is perfect;
the word of the Lord proves true;
he is a shield for all those who take refuge in him."

2 Samuel 22:31 ESV

It's likely that you are well aware of your weaknesses. You know where you fall short and what your limitations are. You might have glaring faults, or you might keep your downfalls hidden. Either way, your humanity cannot be compared to God's perfection. He is always right, good, and true.

God's does not hold his perfection over you. Rather, he provided a way for you to partake of it. Through Christ, you get to experience the perfection of God. In the glory of his love, your weaknesses fade away. Your mistakes and flaws diminish as you turn your eyes to him and are transformed by his mercy and grace. Run to him today and experience the perfection of his presence.

Righteous King, you are better than anyone I've ever known, and I rest in you. Thank you for covering my weaknesses with your love. Transform me in your presence.

ASK AND RECEIVE

"Everyone who asks will receive. The one who searches will find. And everyone who knocks will have the door opened."

LUKE 11:10 NCV

Everything you need can be found in God's presence. The only thing you need to do is ask. When you turn to him for help, you acknowledge who he is and who you are. Your dependence upon him shows an awareness and appreciation for his ability to provide for you.

Bring everything you have to God. Give him your doubts, worries, and fears. Ask him for increased trust, encouragement, and healing. Bring him your questions and humbly ask for answers. Give him your frustrations and expectantly ask him to transform your heart. He will be faithful to provide all you need.

Lord, strengthen my faith when I have doubts. Remind me of your faithful provision. I open my heart to you and offer you everything I have.

GENEROUS LIVING

One person gives freely,
yet gains more;
another withholds what is right,
only to become poor.

PROVERBS 11:24 CSB

When you anxiously hold onto what you have, it shows that you value your control more than God's ability to provide for you. His kingdom doesn't operate the way the world does. In his kingdom, giving away what you have means you will be blessed. He asks you to be generous whether you have a little or a lot.

God's commandments don't produce shame. He leads you gently and equips you to follow him. If you desire to grow in generosity, he will help you. He will soften your heart as you submit to his ways. As you choose to hold your blessings loosely, he will provide what you need.

Great God, I want to be more generous than I currently am. Change my perspective and soften my heart. Help me to take practical steps in generosity today.

SOW INTO FRIENDSHIP

Sweet friendships refresh the soul
and awaken our hearts with joy,
for good friends are like the anointing oil
that yields the fragrant incense of God's presence.

PROVERBS 27:9 TPT

Relationships make life rich. It is a great blessing to be seen, known, and accepted. It is also a gift to learn from the people around you. Each person in your life displays various characteristics of God, and you can glean from them if you pay attention.

Consider the people in your life you are thankful for. Lift them up in prayer and intercede on their behalf. Thank God for their lives and deliberately look for ways to bless them. Encourage them with your words and serve them with your actions. Deliberately sow into your friendships and celebrate the beauty that comes from such sweet fellowship.

Lord, you know all about friendship. You created me to both know others and be known. Thank you for the people who bring refreshing and peace to my life. I'm so grateful for each of them.

FULLY SEEN

All my longings lie open before you, LORD;
my sighing is not hidden from you.

PSALM 38:9 NIV

God sees you just as you are without pretense or misgiving. He is aware of every part of you. He cannot be fooled by any of your attempts to pull yourself together. You don't have to pretend to be happier than you are at any given moment. You can bring your most authentic self into his presence, and he will not turn you away.

God offers you rest and relief in the comforting presence of his Spirit. He reminds you of his all-seeing nature not to shame you but to offer you peace. He longs for you to bring him your tangled heart and let him gently transform it. He doesn't want you to spend your energy trying to fabricate goodness when he offers you an unending supply of grace and mercy.

Lord, I trust that you see my heart as it is, and you meet me where I am. I don't want to hide myself from you. Read my longings and answer the cries of my heart.

FILLED UP

I pray that God, the source of all hope, will fill you completely with joy and peace because you trust in him. Then you will overflow with confident hope through the power of the Holy Spirit.

ROMANS 15:13 NLT

As you trust in the Lord, he fills you completely with his joy and peace. What a promise! He is the source of all hope, not only for you but for the entire world. As God fills you up with his plentiful peace and uplifting joy, you will overflow with confident hope in every area of your life.

As you meet with God today, ask him to renew your hope. The only caveat to his promise of joy and peace is that you trust in him. He doesn't bring up your previous mistakes, and he doesn't ask why it took you so long. He cares more about the surrendered state of your heart than anything else. Run to him with confidence because he will do what he says.

Glorious God, you are the source of all that I need. You see where I am running dry. Fill me up to overflow with your peace, joy, and love today.

COURAGEOUS HOPE

Be strong, and let your heart take courage,
all you who wait for the LORD!

PSALM 31:24 ESV

Why should you take courage in God today? Scripture says that God preserves the faithful. You can be strong because you know God will take care of you. You can have courage because the creator of the universe is on your side.

If you remain faithful to God, he will remain faithful to you. He will not let you down. If your eyes are turned toward him, your feet will not go astray. You can trust him because he has proven himself trustworthy. You can depend on his promises because you know without a shadow of a doubt that he will accomplish them.

Faithful Father, I yield my understanding to you. I know that you are greater than I can imagine. I offer you my heart and life. Fill me with hope as I trust in you.

LIFT YOUR CHIN

"I have redeemed you;
I have called you by name; you are Mine!"

Isaiah 43:1 NASB

When you know that you belong to the King of kings, that truth will filter into every area of your life. It will impact your mindset, relationships, and lifestyle. God has declared who you are and has invited you to live under the banner of his love.

Today, remember that you belong to God and with God. You matter to him, and he is delighted by you. He offers you every benefit that comes from being part of his family. Embrace the truth about who you are. Lift your chin and stand confidently as a child of God.

Redeemer, thank you for embracing me as your own. Thank you for covering my life with the power of your restorative love. You are my home, and I am who you say I am. Father, I delight in you.

COME TO YOUR FATHER

"He arose and came to his father. But when he was still a great way off, his father saw him and had compassion, and ran and fell on his neck and kissed him."

LUKE 15:20 NKJV

In the parable of the prodigal son, Jesus illustrated how loving the Father is. A good father is delighted by the presence of his son. He greets him with joy and acceptance. A good father does not hold his child's mistakes against him, but he extravagantly celebrates each victory.

No matter how much of your inheritance you have squandered, God is waiting to meet you as you turn to him. He has royal robes to wrap around you. He will not ignore you or disown you. He waits patiently for you to approach him. As you come, he runs to meet you while you are still on your way.

Good Father, your mercy is unmatched, and your love is overwhelmingly good. Thank you for embracing me, redeeming me, and calling me your own. I won't stay away from your presence, for you are indescribably kind to me.

SHARE GOOD NEWS

"Go into all the world and preach the gospel to all creation."

MARK 16:15 CSB

Good news is worth sharing; it's worth highlighting and focusing on. Current culture thrives on the focus of bad news, arguments, and disrespectful debates. Instead of falling in line with the world, stand out by declaring the goodness of God. Even when everything seems to be falling apart, God is faithful.

As you turn your eyes toward the truth, God will give you peace and contentment. As your words and actions reflect his love to others, you'll have the satisfaction of knowing you are following his commands. Focus on God's goodness and let your heart rest.

Merciful King, I know that where there are reports of bad news, there is also goodness at work. Your miraculous mercy is always working even through seasons of drought and famine. May I be a bearer of good news no matter what is going on in the world.

WONDERFUL WISDOM

The wisdom that comes from God is first of all pure, then peaceful, gentle, and easy to please. This wisdom is always ready to help those who are troubled and to do good for others. It is always fair and honest.

JAMES 3:17 NCV

God's wisdom is pure, peaceful, gentle, and easy to please. It is honest and ready to help those who are in trouble. It is fair, kind, and generous. If the wisdom you receive or give is anything less than this, it does not come from God.

God gives wisdom to you every time you ask for it. If your life doesn't line up with James' definition of wisdom, all you have to do is ask God for help. He will not turn you away. He readily transforms your heart whenever you turn to him.

God, I want to be consumed with your wisdom instead of my own opinions or the opinions of others. I want to walk in the freedom of your love that leads with kindness, honesty, peace, and joy.

FEED YOUR MIND

Perfect, absolute peace surrounds those
whose imaginations are consumed with you;
they confidently trust in you.

Isaiah 26:3 TPT

When your imagination is consumed with the truth of who God is, you can rest in the perfect peace of his loyal love. God is faithful, just, and merciful. He never changes his mind, and he is always reliable.

You can direct your imagination toward the Lord in a manner of ways. You can read Scripture, listen to worship music, dwell on his character, or engage with him in prayer. Whichever option you choose, deliberately fill your mind with truth today. As you seek him, your heart will grow in hope and your faith will be strengthened.

Lord, I direct my attention to you over and over again. Each time I do, expand my understanding of you, even as my imagination stretches to contain more of who you are. I will feast on the power of your unchanging character and meditate on your mercy.

STEP BY STEP

"Blessed rather are those who hear the word of God and obey it."

LUKE 11:28 NIV

It is not enough to simply know the truth. Your belief in God must go beyond knowing and grow roots deep within your heart. Your life must reflect his character and display evidence of being submitted to his ways.

Obeying God's Word requires humility and patience. It takes time to learn and integrate things into your life. Don't be discouraged by your perceived timeline. Rather, humble yourself daily before God and allow him to do the work of transforming your heart. This is the foundation for true obedience.

Gracious Jesus, thank you for your wisdom and patience. As I put your ways into practice in my life, direct me on the path of your choosing. I follow you because I know that you are the way, the truth, and the life.

GOOD CONNECTIONS

Every time I think of you, I give thanks to my God.

PHILIPPIANS 1:3 NLT

It's easy to be disappointed by the things you don't have. On some days falling into discouragement and comparison feels natural. However, if you take time to account for the good things in life, an attitude of gratitude can lift your spirit and rejuvenate your hope.

There are surely people who have had a positive impact on your life. Celebrate their influence and thank God for their presence in your life. Notice how God has provided for you through various people and open your eyes to the blessings you've received. Allow God to soften your heart and remind you the good things in your life.

My God, thank you for the wonderful people you have placed in my life to bring encouragement, hope, and comfort. I cannot thank you enough for the power of their impact in my life.

MARCH

God is our refuge and strength,
a helper who is always found
in times of trouble.

Psalm 46:1 CSB

GIFT OF TODAY

This is the day which the LORD has made;
Let us rejoice and be glad in it.

PSALM 118:24 NASB

Today is a gift from God, and you get to decide how you will receive it. Take a moment before your schedule carries you away and quiet your heart before him. Give him the chance to set the tone for the rest of your day.

In his presence, God will give you everything you need. He knows exactly what the next 24 hours will look like. He is fully capable of equipping you to handle whatever comes your way. Allow him to strengthen you and adjust your attitude. Start your day from a foundation of thanksgiving and trust. Move forward with the expectation that God will take care of you.

Faithful One, thank you for today; it is a fresh start and a reason to give thanks. I want to rejoice in the goodness of your presence all day long.

BEAUTIFUL MESS

"I will save the lame
and gather the outcast,
and I will change their shame into praise
and renown in all the earth."

ZEPHANIAH 3:19 ESV

God is worthy of your trust. He remembers every promise he has ever made, and he follows through on each one. He will deal with the oppressors of this world. He saves the lame, gathers the outcast, and turns your shame into praise. He is wonderful in all he does.

Whatever hard circumstances you are dealing with, know that God is with you. He sees you, and he will fight for you. He is capable of creating beauty from the messiest parts of your life. There is nothing that he cannot do. Rest in his presence and dwell on the faithfulness of his character.

Redeemer, thank you for the hope of your salvation. I trust you to come through for me in practical and supernatural ways. I choose to follow you because you are worthy.

THE RIGHT MOMENT

Let the wicked one abandon his way
and the sinful one his thoughts;
let him return to the LORD,
so he may have compassion on him,
and to our God, for he will freely forgive.

ISAIAH 55:7 CSB

It is never too late to turn to God. It is always the right moment to come to him. No matter how short or long it's been, the Lord welcomes you with an overflowing heart of mercy. He longs to lift the burdens from your shoulders and forgive what you have trouble letting go of.

God is a tremendously good Father. He is full of kindness and compassion. He has strategies to help you overcome the hurdles in your life. He has comfort for your pain, strength for your weakness, and hope for your despair. Don't stay away from him when you can be engulfed in his loving embrace today.

Merciful Father, I cannot begin to thank you for your kindness toward me. I love you, and I trust you. As I come to you, lift my heavy burdens I offer and wash me anew in the living waters of your presence.

PERFECT JUDGE

"The LORD does not see as man sees; for man looks at the outward appearance, but the LORD looks at the heart."

1 SAMUEL 16:7 NKJV

God is the perfect judge because he sees through outer appearances into the intentions of the heart. He knows what each person is made of. He sees each circumstance with perfect clarity. He navigates nuance expertly and with perfect wisdom. Everything he does is good and right.

Regardless of how well put-together you feel, God does not base his opinion of you on how you look. He is not impressed or deterred by your stature, abilities, or talents. You don't have to strive to find your place because you have already been established in Christ. He is far more concerned with the state of your heart than anything else.

Lord Jesus, your ways, thoughts, and judgments are better than those of this world. I don't want to impress others only to find that I've lost myself in the process. Ground me in your love that I may flourish as I was always meant to.

LIKE A CHILD

"Let the little children come to me. Don't stop them, because the kingdom of God belongs to people who are like these children."

LUKE 18:16 NCV

Consider what it means to be childlike. They are open, vulnerable, and curious. They can be inquisitive and hyper-focused. They can be silly and creative. A child's faith is steadfast and sure. They aren't easily swayed from their passions and pursuits.

Jesus welcomes you just as he welcomed the little children. He loves the messiness of authenticity. You don't have to dress up or act differently. You don't have to pretend to understand what you have not yet learned. You don't have to silence your questions. Simply come to him, for he welcomes you with open arms.

Wonderful Jesus, thank you for welcoming me as I am. I want to allow my childlike curiosity and wonder to grow. I am yours, and I come running to you today.

WITH PURPOSE

We have become his poetry, a re-created people that will fulfill the destiny he has given each of us, for we are joined to Jesus, the Anointed One. Even before we were born, God planned in advance our destiny and the good works we would do to fulfill it!

EPHESIANS 2:10 TPT

You were created with purpose. You were knit together with creativity and intention. Each one of your days has been laid out before you by your kind and wise Creator. He knows what the entirety of your life looks like.

The trajectory of your life is not a secret. Before you were born God planned your days and filled them with good works for you to do. You might not know the whole picture, but you can trust that it is good. You can take each step with confidence because you know that God is aware of you and will provide for you.

Creator, thank you for designing me with a purpose. I am not a mistake, and I don't have to be like anyone else around me. Thank you for the power of your love that liberates me to live fully as the person you've created me to be.

EVERY GIFT

Every good and perfect gift is from above, coming down from the Father of the heavenly lights, who does not change like shifting shadows.

JAMES 1:17 NIV

Every good and perfect gift is from above. Every miracle of mercy in your life comes directly from God's hands. From the food on your table to the breath in your lungs, every blessing comes from him. There is no reason too big or too small to praise him.

Practice noticing the good today. It's easy to let negativity cloud your vision, but it takes effort and intention to find reasons to be thankful. The more you pay attention to God's gifts, the more you will see them everywhere. As you praise him, he will open your eyes to the vast tapestry of mercy he has woven in your life and in the lives of those around you.

Good Father, I humble my heart before you knowing I have so much to learn still. Teach me your ways. I want to know who you truly are. Open my eyes to the enormity of your goodness in my life.

LOVE WELL

"Do to others as you would like them to do to you."

Luke 6:31 NLT

When you are tempted to be hasty and retaliate against those who have hurt you, remember what Jesus said. It's not always easy to treat others as you want to be treated, but it is always worth it. Following Jesus' instructions always results in blessing.

You can't love others perfectly, and Jesus doesn't expect you to. He asks you to have a willing and submissive heart. Even when you fail, you can repair and restore relationships through humility and forgiveness. A soft heart that is committed to love covers over a multitude of weaknesses and misgivings.

Jesus, help me to walk in the light of your love. I choose to follow you and adopt your ways because they are right and true. Give me grace to lay down my preferences for the sake of others.

HOPE EXPANDED

I pray that the eyes of your heart may be enlightened, so that you will know what is the hope of His calling, what are the riches of the glory of His inheritance in the saints.

EPHESIANS 1:18 NASB

As the eyes of your heart open in revelatory understanding, your hope will expand. You will catch glimpses of the glorious goodness that awaits you in the fullness of Christ's kingdom. Every sacrifice and surrender will be worth it.

The fulfillment of God's promises will be so much better than you can imagine. If you are struggling to see the purpose of your life or the value of following Jesus, ask God to open your eyes. He will gladly give you a glimpse of what's to come. He will faithfully remind you of the hope of his calling. When you are weary, he will carry you through.

Great One, open the eyes of my heart. Fill me with wonder and awe. You are glorious, and I know one day I will see you fully. I wait and long for that day to come. In the meantime, show me more of who you are.

POWER OF FAITH

"Truly, I say to you, if you have faith like a grain of mustard seed, you will say to this mountain, 'Move from here to there,' and it will move, and nothing will be impossible for you."

MATTHEW 17:20 ESV

You don't need a large amount of faith to make a difference. You don't need to know the details of the future in order to move ahead one step. Jesus said that even the smallest seed of faith could move a mountain from its place. Don't underestimate the power of faith, no matter how small it is.

God might ask you to do extravagant things for his kingdom. He might ask you to take massive risks or do something that scares you. He might also ask you to faithfully tend to something you consider boring. Your faith can be stretched by the mundane as much as the monumental. In every circumstance, trust that God will move as you call on him.

Faithful One, I'm so glad you don't require more of me than I am able to give. Strengthen my faith however you see fit. Speak to me, and I will listen.

VALUABLE STORIES

Whatever was written in the past was written for our instruction, so that we may have hope through endurance and through the encouragement from the Scriptures.

ROMANS 15:4 CSB

When you approach life as if you have to figure everything out on your own, you miss out on the wisdom of those who have gone before you. Generational community is so important. Those who have already lived their own struggles can offer wisdom and guidance. You don't have to begin from scratch.

God has given you a beautiful gift in the stories of others. You can be encouraged by their triumphs and learn from their mistakes. The hope of Christ has been interwoven in his people's lives from generation to generation. Approach the Word with an open heart and find the encouragement you need. Read the testimonies of other believers and allow God's faithfulness to them inspire you.

Almighty God, I don't want to struggle to understand what you so willingly teach. Open my heart and understanding as I partner with you and your purposes.

EACH MORNING

I have hope when I think of this:
the LORD's love never ends;
his mercies never stop.
They are new every morning.

LAMENTATIONS 3:21-23 NCV

Today is a new day. Allow that to sink in. Let the regrets of yesterday fade away as you focus your attention on the fresh mercy of God. He has everything you need. Fill up on his grace, peace, and joy. He is overflowing with kindness, and he does not wane in strength.

Give yesterday's concerns to the Lord. He knows exactly what to do with them. Instead of dwelling on what cannot be changed, ask him how to move forward. He will lead you with gentleness and wisdom. If you let him, he will direct your steps and make your path straight.

Merciful One, thank you for always knowing exactly what I need at any given moment. Give me a fresh revelation of your mercy. Take the burden of yesterday's struggles and equip me to face whatever comes my way.

SAFE REFUGE

Preserve me, O God,
For in You I put my trust.

Psalm 16:1 NKJV

God is a safe place in every kind of trouble. As you run to him, he becomes your refuge. No matter what happens, no one can take away his prevalent peace. No one can remove you from his love. Put your faith in him and he will preserve you.

What do you need God's preservation for? Are there struggles or temptations that you feel vulnerable toward? You can trust God's Spirit to help you. Even when you fall, the grace of God is your landing pad. Don't let shame, fear, or regret keep you from coming to him. He is patient with you, and he is able to empower you to stand.

God, I put my trust in you. When I am afraid and weak, I run to you. Surround me with your presence and settle my heart in the clarity of your love.

EXPERT HEALER

He heals the wounds of every shattered heart.

PSALM 147:3 TPT

You cannot escape the pain of heartbreak in this life. You cannot outrun grief, and you cannot avoid suffering. Until you see God face to face, you will have to deal with pain. It's inevitable. While you can't control your circumstances, you can control how you react to them.

Allow pain to drive into God's arms. When grief is too much to bear, run to your Father. When suffering seems senseless and overwhelming, cast your burdens upon him. He is the healer of every broken heart. He won't patch you back together haphazardly. Rather, he will expertly mend your deepest wounds.

Healer, you are the one who knit me together in the first place, and you can knit my shattered heart together again. I trust you for healing when I need it most.

COVENANT LOVE

"Know therefore that the LORD your God is God; he is the faithful God, keeping his covenant of love to a thousand generations of those who love him and keep his commandments."

DEUTERONOMY 7:9 NIV

Promises are made and broken all the time, but God never breaks a promise. His nature doesn't allow it. He is faithful, merciful, and just. God keeps his covenant of love, and he will never forget what he has said, nor will he change his mind.

God's faithfulness to you does not depend on your ability to be faithful. He knows that you will make mistakes and sometimes wander down the wrong path. He isn't intimidated by your faults or frustrated by your weaknesses. His faithfulness is greater than your shortcomings. Let this glorious truth draw you closer to his heart. Let his covenant love spur you toward greater affection for your Maker.

Powerful One, thank you for the strength of your covenant love. Remind me of your faithfulness. Help me keep my eyes on your steadiness rather than my own shortcomings.

GOD'S STORY

God has made everything beautiful for its own time. He has planted eternity in the human heart, but even so, people cannot see the whole scope of God's work from beginning to end.

Ecclesiastes 3:11 NLT

You cannot know the scope of God's work in the world, but you can certainly find yourself within his mercy. Even when the world feels chaotic and nothing makes sense, there is always hope. Keep your eyes on him and expect him to keep his promises.

As long as you have breath there are sunsets to chase and loved ones to embrace. Instead of focusing on what you don't have or what isn't right, notice the beauty in what God has done and is doing in your life. You are part of his glorious story, and he will not let you down.

God, I trust you even when the world feels chaotic. I trust you even when I don't understand my own circumstances. You are faithful and worthy of all my praise.

NOT MINE

"LORD our God, all this abundance that we have provided to build You a house for Your holy name, it is from Your hand, and all is Yours."

1 CHRONICLES 29:16 NASB

If everything finds its source in God, then everything belongs to him. You can hold onto what isn't yours, or you can experience the joy of generosity. As you open your heart and hands, you honor God by surrendering your many gifts back to him.

There is freedom to be found in generosity. As you recognize that you are a steward of God's blessings, you can also recognize that he is responsible for them. He faithfully takes care of each of his children. He is the one who provides for you, and he is capable of giving you exactly what you need.

Creator, I don't want to live as a mindless consumer of things. I want to partner with your heart and purposes. Thank for each opportunity I have to be generous. You have blessed me, and I will bless others in your name.

DELIGHTFUL OBEDIENCE

This is the love of God, that we keep his commandments. And his commandments are not burdensome.

1 JOHN 5:3 ESV

The law of God's love is not burdensome. It actually becomes a delight as you live it out. It won't always feel easy, but God's grace empowers you to choose his ways, for they are loving and beneficial to all.

As you approach your workload today, what if you looked for ways to infuse it with love? How could you delight in your tasks instead of dreading them? The love of God isn't reserved for spiritual tasks. It reaches every part of your life.

Gracious God, I want to know the delight of following you and partnering with you. Shift my perspective and help me see the joy of being obedient to your ways.

TRUE IDENTITY

You are a chosen people, royal priests, a holy nation, a people for God's own possession. You were chosen to tell about the wonderful acts of God, who called you out of darkness into his wonderful light.

1 PETER 2:9 NCV

When you chose to follow Jesus, he gave you a new name. He called you his own, and he carved your identity into his hands. Through Christ you are accepted and redeemed. You are set apart, protected, and valued.

No matter what the world says about you, God says you are his prized possession. Even when other people don't see you rightly, God says you are his own. Through Christ he pulled you out of darkness and into his glorious light. Rejoice in your glorious identity today.

Glorious One, thank you for the light of your love that shines brightly in my life. Give me confidence to be exactly who you created me to be.

REWARD OF PATIENCE

Those who trust in the Lord
will renew their strength;
they will soar on wings like eagles;
they will run and not become weary,
they will walk and not faint.

ISAIAH 40:31 CSB

You can't speed up seasons of waiting. You can't avoid them or scheme your way out of them. The only solution for waiting is endurance. You simply have to persevere day by day. That does not mean that waiting is wasted. God can do wonderful things while you wait on him.

With each passing day, you can rest in God's presence. You can find peace, joy, and strength despite circumstances that don't change. You can strengthen your faith and anchor your hope to the promises of God. When you trust him in the waiting, the reward is even sweeter.

Faithful One, thank you for your promised strength. When I am weak, you are powerful. When I am disappointed, you are confident and sure. Help me lean on you in seasons of waiting.

BELOVED CHILD

I am my beloved's,
And his desire is toward me.

SONG OF SOLOMON 7:10 NKJV

When you come to Christ, you are no longer on your own. You belong to him. When you yield your life to his leadership, he welcomes you as a friend and beloved child. You are not an outsider or a stranger at his table. You are the delight of his heart and the object of his affection.

When you are secure in your identity, your actions will reflect it. True confidence doesn't come from outward appearances, skills and talents, or physical circumstances. True confidence comes from knowing who you are and who God is. Let his love permeate your heart and ground you in truth.

Jesus, thank you for loving me so fully. There isn't anyone else who loves me as wonderfully as you do. I am overwhelmed by the kindness and goodness of your heart.

PRINCE OF PEACE

In the middle of the night I awake to give thanks to you because of all your revelation-light; so right and true!

PSALM 119:62 TPT

Have you ever woken up in the middle of the night full of worry? Your mind feels frantic and worst-case scenarios plague your thoughts. Everything seems worse and less manageable in the dark. It's not a coincidence that Scripture addresses this. God knew that you might feel vulnerable and alone at night.

The next time you wake up unexpectedly speak peace to your soul. Direct your thoughts and attention to the Prince of Peace. Give thanks for his glorious light that cannot be extinguished no matter how dark it is. Turn your worries over to him and rest in the safety of his presence.

Lord, thank you for the truth that I am not a victim to my mind. Help me direct my attention and thoughts toward you. I am so thankful for the power of your love that meets me and brings peace that passes understanding.

FULLY EQUIPPED

"Love your enemies, do good to them, and lend to them without expecting to get anything back. Then your reward will be great, and you will be children of the Most High, because he is kind to the ungrateful and wicked."

LUKE 6:35 NIV

Perhaps the most difficult command in Scripture is to love your enemies. God doesn't just ask you to put up with your enemies but to do good to them and be generous toward them. He is asking you to do something that feels counterintuitive and sometimes even painful.

Rest assured that God will never leave you unequipped. He has given you everything you need to follow his instructions. The mercy, grace, and kindness he has poured upon your life are more than enough to share. He knows exactly how difficult it can be to love your enemies, but he is by your side ready to strengthen you whenever you need it.

Merciful Jesus, I want to grow in my capacity to love. Help me stop making excuses for my biases, hate, and stinginess. I want to be more like you.

IN EVERY SEASON

"Because of God's tender mercy,
the morning light from heaven is about to break upon us,
to give light to those who sit in darkness
and in the shadow of death,
to guide us to the path of peace."

LUKE 1:78-79 NLT

No dark night lasts forever. Winter does not draw out in endless measure. Just as the seasons shift and change, so does your life. Difficulties will come and go. No matter what you are walking through right now, God never changes. He is always full of light, hope, mercy, and peace.

In every season of the soul, God is your light. Look to him for guidance, protection, warmth, and encouragement. When your path is dimly lit and you can't tell which way to go, ask him. When you're alone in the dark and your burdens are heavy, call out to him. In his mercy he will not abandon you.

Reliable One, transform my heart with your peace today. I want to rest in the knowledge that you are with me. Remind me of your faithfulness when I am struggling.

IN YOUR LANGUAGE

As He was going along by the Sea of Galilee, He saw Simon and Andrew, the brother of Simon, casting a net in the sea; for they were fishermen. And Jesus said to them, "Follow Me, and I will make you become fishers of people." Immediately they left their nets and followed Him.

MARK 1:16-18 NASB

Jesus spoke to people through stories and metaphors that made sense to the listeners. He asked Simon and Andrew to become fishers of men because he knew they would understand the concept of fishing. He met them where they were and invited them to follow him.

God is capable of communicating with you in a way you understand. He does not hold his instructions over your head to be unreachable or unachievable. He is thoughtful toward you. He knows how to call you in the language of your heart. He invites you to partner with him as he moves on earth. All you have to do is respond.

God, thank you for speaking to me personally in a way I understand. Draw me closer to you and equip me to do your will on the earth.

OPPORTUNITY FOR GROWTH

Do everything without grumbling and arguing, so that you may be blameless and pure, children of God who are faultless in a crooked and perverted generation, among whom you shine like stars in the world.

PHILIPPIANS 2:14-15 CSB

Complaining can be an indication of resentment or unmet expectations. When you find yourself grumbling or arguing with others, ask yourself why with curiosity. You don't have to be flooded with guilt and shame. Instead, consider your actions an invitation to bring your weaknesses to the Lord.

Feeling like a failure will keep you from personal growth and intimacy with God. Guilt and repentance are two different things. Guilt drives you toward introspection and self-examination, while repentance drives you to humbly lean on God and make changes through the power of his grace.

Wise God, you always understand my actions even when I don't. Help me see opportunities for repentance and growth. Give me grace to turn to you when I notice my mistakes.

BETTER TO BUILD

The wise woman builds her house,
But the foolish pulls it down with her hands.

PROVERBS 14:1 NKJV

Walking in wisdom makes you a builder rather than a destroyer. You build your family, life, and community with encouragement, truth, and love. A foolish person tears down their own life by refusing to grow, change, and accept God's grace.

It is better to be a builder than a destroyer. There is always room in your life for growth. In your quiet time with God, ask him to lead you down the path of his choosing. As you walk with him, he will highlight areas of growth and equip you to follow his leadership. Trusting his direction isn't always comfortable, but it is always worth it.

Creator, even in the rubble of destruction, you are always building a new thing. You bring life wherever you go. May I partner with your heart and build something that lasts.

GENTLE ANSWER

A gentle answer will calm a person's anger,
but an unkind answer will cause more anger.

PROVERBS 15:1 NCV

The book of Proverbs is full of wisdom for interacting with other people. It also gives you a glimpse of God's character. He doesn't ask his children to behave in a way that is contradictory of his own nature. Therefore, if Scripture teaches you to stay calm in the midst of frustration, you can assume that when you are angry, God speaks to you gently.

When you go to God with your intense emotions, he does not match your energy. He does not respond with impatience or unkindness. He is the epitome of grace, peace, and mercy at all times. His presence is the perfect place to take your untamed emotions. Run to him for refuge and allow him to calm your storms.

Lord, thank you for being gentle with me when I am overwhelmed, angry, and upset. Teach me how to be more like you. Help me to reflect your character in the way I respond to others.

EMBODIMENT OF TRUTH

God is not man, that he should lie,
or a son of man, that he should change his mind.
Has he said, and will he not do it?
Or has he spoken, and will he not fulfill it?

NUMBERS 23:19 ESV

Not only does God tell the truth, but he is the truth. There isn't a shadow of doubt, manipulation, or deceit in him. God is pure light and love. He is the true source of wisdom, power, and strength. He is faithful, and he follows through on his word.

Even when the people around you can't be trusted, God's character is reliable. Even when the world feels chaotic and you can't get your head above water, God's Word remains unshaken. In all circumstances he is your refuge and strength. Look to him in every trial and triumph, for he is the same yesterday, today, and forever.

God, thank you for the power of your love that stands the test of time. You do not lie or cheat or steal. You are pure, true, and faithful. I trust you.

PROMISED PEACE

If while we were still enemies, God fully reconciled us to himself through the death of his Son, then something greater than friendship is ours. Now that we are at peace with God, and because we share in his resurrection life, how much more we will be rescued from sin's dominion!

ROMANS 5:10 TPT

Through Jesus, you have peace with God. Nothing stands between you and a flourishing relationship with your Maker. When you feel distant, ashamed, or inadequate, remember that truth matters more than feelings. You can lean on God's Word rather than letting your life be dictated by your emotions.

Soak up the peace of God's presence and fill your heart with the Word. Dwell on the truth and it will be like a life preserver when storms come. You will stay afloat because you are confident in God's ability to rescue you. You won't be overcome because you trust God to come through for you.

Jesus, thank you for being the Prince of Peace. You don't just offer mercy and hope, but peace that settles my heart in your presence. Thank you.

STRONG AND EMPOWERED

The grace of God has appeared that offers salvation to all people. It teaches us to say "No" to ungodliness and worldly passions, and to live self-controlled, upright and Godly lives in this present age.

Titus 2:11-12 NIV

With the grace of God at hand, you can choose to say no to the things of this world. When you live by your own strength it feels impossible to overcome sin. When you lean on the Lord, he gives you exactly what you need to be victorious against temptation.

If you let him, God will actively transform your life. He will lead, guide, and equip you to walk along a godly path. He will empower you to make wise choices, and he will strengthen you when you are weak. He is well aware of the challenges you face, and he promises to be with you every step of the way.

Gracious God, I cannot begin to thank you for your grace that empowers me to live with intention. Thank you for saving me; thank you for teaching me and guiding me. Give me strength to live according to your will.

APRIL

Better a day in your courts
than a thousand anywhere else.

Psalm 84:10 CSB

STEADY GAZE

"All this may seem impossible to you now, a small remnant of God's people. But is it impossible for me?" says the LORD of Heaven's Armies.

ZECHARIAH 8:6 NLT

It may seem foolish to hope for God's promises to be fulfilled. Worldly events might sway your confidence, but God is able to do far more than you could ever plan or imagine. He holds the trajectory of the world firmly in his hands. He knows exactly what he is doing, and his ways are perfect.

Instead of frantically looking around at grim circumstances, turn your eyes to the Lord. Gaze at him steadily and allow him to direct your steps. When you put your faith in him above all else, the disappointing actions of others become far less catastrophic. The peace you might get from worldly circumstances aligning nicely cannot compare with the peace that he offers you.

Mighty Creator, there is nothing you cannot do. I trust your wisdom, timing, and plan. I trust that you will follow through on every one of your promises.

CHOSEN AND APPOINTED

"You did not choose Me but I chose you, and appointed you that you would go and bear fruit, and that your fruit would remain, so that whatever you ask of the Father in My name He may give to you."

JOHN 15:16 NASB

The Lord your God has chosen you and appointed you to bear the fruit of his kingdom in your life. This is not a weighty task but a light one. As you yield to his leadership, he transforms you in the light of his presence. He is the one who does the work.

You don't need to strive or simply do better. God doesn't expect you to grit your teeth through life while feeling like a constant failure. He wants you to confidently ask for what you need. He wants to you trust him as your kind and generous Father. Through Christ, he gives you everything you need to live according to his will.

Faithful One, thank you for all that you have done and are doing in my life. Your perfect peace, jubilant joy, refreshing love, constant kindness, persistent patience, and uplifting hope keep me coming back to you.

JOY OF PARTNERSHIP

From ancient times no one has heard,
no one has listened to,
no eye has seen any God except you
who acts on behalf of the one who waits for him.

Isaiah 64:4 CSB

God is greater than you can imagine. He is not bound by your understanding or limitations. He cannot be controlled or manipulated, yet he delights in walking with you. Even though you are massively unmatched when it comes to skill or ability, he is happy to partner with you.

God doesn't need your talents to accomplish his will. There is no pressure for you to perform a certain way in order to qualify for kingdom work. The most important part of working with God is having a heart that is submitted to him and eyes that are focused on him. Wait humbly and patiently for his instructions and he will not turn you away.

Mighty God, thank you for the honor of partnering with you. Thank you for compensating for my weaknesses and for using me to accomplish your will. Give me grace to humbly follow you.

GIFT OF THE SPIRIT

"The Helper, the Holy Spirit, whom the Father will send in My name, He will teach you all things, and bring to your remembrance all things that I said to you."

JOHN 14:26 NKJV

You are never alone. When you surrendered your life to God you were given the gift of the Holy Spirit. He is your helper, guide, and encourager in all circumstances. He speaks to you about God's wisdom and character, and he reminds you of the truth.

The Holy Spirit is one of your greatest assets. As you spend time with God even now, remember that your interactions with him aren't limited to your quiet time. The Spirit is with you at all times. He walks with you throughout your day and empowers you to honor God in all you do.

Lord, thank you for your present and sufficient grace, mercy, and kindness. Thank you for your Spirit that dwells within me and guides me with your perfect wisdom. I am so grateful to be known and led by you.

REMAIN IN LOVE

Keep yourselves in the love of God, waiting for the mercy of our Lord Jesus Christ that leads to eternal life.

JUDE 1:21 ESV

What does it look like to remain in the love of God? Like any habit, it takes intentionality and consistency. The more you remind yourself of the truth, the more quickly you will recall it in times of need. The more you cultivate intimacy with God, the stronger your relationship becomes.

Every time you look to God, your faith grows. Even the smallest glance increases your trust in him. Keeping yourself in the love of God isn't supposed to be a burdensome or impossible task. It's as simple as looking in his direction and keeping your heart soft to his commands.

Everlasting God, thank you for the limitless love you pour out on me. I want to feast each day on your mercy, receiving all that I need from you alone. Help me cultivate the habit of remaining in your love.

HEAVENLY HOMELAND

Our homeland is in heaven, and we are waiting for our Savior, the Lord Jesus Christ, to come from heaven.

PHILIPPIANS 3:20 NCV

When the world is a mess and you feel out of place, may you remember the truth that Paul spoke in today's verse. Your homeland is in heaven. This is the hope that tethers you to God's promise of redemption. When you are discouraged by what's happening around you, remember that you don't belong here.

The trials you experience will not last forever. The injustice you witness will one day be made right. Instead of being discouraged by the mess you see around you, let it drive you to wait on the Lord with greater hope and anticipation.

Heavenly Father, thank you for the promise of your kingdom coming to earth. I want to know your presence even now as I wait. You are my hope, my strength, and my song.

GLORIOUS VICTORY

Even in the midst of all these things, we triumph over them all, for God has made us to be more than conquerors, and his demonstrated love is our glorious victory over everything.

ROMANS 8:37 TPT

Your greatest victory is found in what Christ has already done for you. He has demonstrated the lengths of his love, and the power of his resurrection has conquered every enemy you might face. Nothing can come across your path that is too much for you to overcome.

Knowing you are liberated in love means you can walk with steady and confident steps. You don't have to fear the unknown or worry about what tomorrow might bring. No matter what happens, God is with you. In every circumstance, his love is your glorious victory.

Victorious One, thank you for the power to overcome. Give me confidence in your strength over my own. May I run to you at the first sign of trouble, trusting in your ability to carry me through.

ROOTED IN LOVE

The righteous will flourish like a palm tree,
they will grow like a cedar of Lebanon.

PSALM 92:12 NIV

If you have surrendered your life to Jesus, his righteousness has become your own. In other words, you are perfect despite your imperfections. Through him you will flourish like a well-nourished tree. You will grow strong and steady as your roots grow deeply into God's love.

You can expect God to do good things in your life. You can expect him to cause you to flourish and thrive in any circumstance. This doesn't mean that each day will look exactly how you want, but it does mean that God's life-giving love will transform you more into his likeness as time goes by.

God, you are the reason I can be strong. When I feel weak, help me remember that I am rooted in your love. Keep me steady when storms come and help me find my confidence in you.

IN GOD'S HANDS

I prayed to the LORD, and he answered me.
He freed me from all my fears.
Those who look to him for help will be radiant with joy.

PSALM 34:4-5 NLT

God is aware of you, and he is concerned with the matters that concern you. Instead of letting fear overtake your heart and mind, actively give your fears to God. He promises to give you freedom and joy in exchange for trusting him.

Take time today to examine your heart. What are you afraid of right now? What are you worried about? Through prayer, give your fears to God. Speak them out loud or write them down. When they threaten to rise up during the day, remind yourself that you have already surrendered them, and they are in God's hands now.

Lord, I need your intervention in my life. The fears that threaten to overtake my heart and mind don't give relief, but I know that you do. I trust you with my worries because you are faithful to take care of me.

TIME TO RISE

A righteous person falls seven times and rises again,
But the wicked stumble in time of disaster.

PROVERBS 24:16 NASB

While you might feel like your failures are too many to count, they are not what defines you. Your ability to rise again matters so much more than how many times you fall. Perseverance and fortitude are far more important than perfection.

Knowing that God does not expect you be perfect can empower you to let go of your own need for perfection. Instead of being brutally judgmental of yourself, soften your heart and cultivate the skill of teachability and humility. Lean on the Lord in your weakness and allow him to graciously lift you up whenever you falter.

Spirit, I don't want to wallow in defeat or failure, and I don't want to get lost in fear, shame, or hopelessness. As I look to you, I rise in your mercy. You lift me up. Thank you.

TARRY WITH GOD

When He saw the multitudes, He was moved with compassion for them, because they were weary and scattered, like sheep having no shepherd.

MATTHEW 9:36 NKJV

Jesus had compassion on those who were weary. Since he is a perfect reflection of the Father, you can believe that God has compassion on you when you are weary. He longs to be your Shepherd who comforts and encourages you whenever you need it.

When you are weary and feeling like a lost sheep, look to the Shepherd. Turn toward him with the expectation that he will faithfully provide for you. He will not turn you away, and he will not lead you astray. The most effective act of self-care you can do is to tarry in the presence of God. Nothing else will renew your spirit like he can.

Compassionate One, thank you for your faithful provision. Thank you for renewing my spirit when I am weary. Lead me and I will follow wherever you go.

A SOFT HEART

"Judge not, and you will not be judged; condemn not, and you will not be condemned; forgive, and you will be forgiven."

LUKE 6:37 ESV

The judgmental will know judgment, and those who condemn others will themselves find that condemnation is thrown their way. However, those who choose humility and forgiveness will find themselves forgiven. Each of these actions begins in the heart.

There is so much freedom to be found in refusing to judge others. Being overly concerned with the actions of others can be exhausting. It takes time and emotional energy to constantly evaluate whether or not other people are doing the right thing. Instead, allow Christ's love to set you free from the desire to micromanage the holiness of others. Allow your heart to be softened and turn your energy toward your own relationship with Jesus.

Father, I don't want to be filled with bitterness or unforgiveness. Give me grace to focus on my relationship with you rather than the actions of others. Soften my heart and help me cultivate humility in my life.

ABIDE

"I am the vine, you are the branches; the one who remains in Me, and I in him bears much fruit, for apart from Me you can do nothing."

John 15:5 CSB

Jesus described himself as a vine and his Father as the one tending to the branches. This illustrates that Jesus is your source of life while the Father prunes and provides for you. As you abide in the vine, you place your life in their expert care.

You abide in Christ by following his lead, adopting his ways, and staying open to implementing Scripture in your life. The more you turn your attention toward him, the more natural it becomes to stay engaged with him. He is your home, your source of life, and your refuge. Everything you need flows from him, and you bear the fruit of his kingdom as you are nourished by him.

Christ, you are the source of all that I need. Help me remain connected to you through your Spirit. Thank you for grafting me into your kingdom and sharing your life with me.

START NOW

Those who wait for perfect weather will never plant seeds; those who look at every cloud will never harvest crops.

ECCLESIASTES 11:4 NCV

If you know the pull of procrastination, then you know the feeling of shame and guilt that can accompany it. Guilt doesn't propel you into action; it only keeps you stuck in the cycle of putting off until tomorrow what could be done today. Instead of beating yourself up for wasting time, approach each moment as a fresh start.

Is there something you've been putting off? How can you take some small steps to accomplish what's before you? You don't have to know how everything will work out, but you can make meaningful progress as you tackle it bit by bit. As you prioritize progress over perfection, you'll experience the satisfaction of a job well done.

Lord, I don't want to keep putting things off for tomorrow when I don't even know how many tomorrows I will have. Give me grace, wisdom, and persistence as I take steps to start today.

SWEET AROMA

Continue to walk surrendered to the extravagant love of Christ, for he surrendered his life as a sacrifice for us. His great love for us was pleasing to God, like an aroma of adoration—a sweet healing fragrance.

Ephesians 5:2 TPT

When you think of the idea of surrendering, you might think about giving up or handing over control. When it comes to giving your life to God, surrendering is not the same thing as quitting. Surrendering to God is an act of wisdom, strength, and faith.

When you trust God with your life, you actively acknowledge his greatness. As you yield to his love, you position yourself to receive the abundant gifts he gives his children. He doesn't ask you to surrender and then leave you empty handed. Rather, he draws you along his path and empowers you every step of the way.

Lord, I surrender to your love today. May its power infuse every part of me. May my thoughts and actions be honoring to you. I offer you my life and everything I have.

HEIRS OF THE PROMISE

If you belong to Christ, then you are Abraham's seed, and heirs according to the promise.

Galatians 3:29 NIV

There is no division between the children of God. There are no distinctions or second-class citizens in his kingdom. Everyone has equal access to the promises of God. Society likes to create divisions and apply labels, but God does not. He doesn't care about your birthplace, ethnicity, or social status.

Sometimes laying down your biases takes real effort and intention. We all have ways of thinking that are incorrect in some way. Humbly offer your tendencies to the Lord and allow him to transform your heart and mind. His love is extravagant and offered abundantly to all who seek it. Lay down your biases and preferences and treat everyone with the dignity and respect they find in Christ.

Christ Jesus, help me to be more open and welcoming of those who are different than me. I want to expand in love instead of shrinking in fear. Give me grace to love without distinction.

CONFIDENT ASSURANCE

What should we say about this? If God is for us, no one can defeat us.

ROMANS 8:31 NCV

You will be overwhelmed if you spend all your energy looking at the problems ahead of you. Focusing on your struggles will only fill you with fear, anxiety, and worry. God doesn't want you to trade your peace in an effort to manage situations that are out of your control anyway.

Instead of dwelling on possible worst-case scenarios, you can recognize your challenges and direct your attention to God. If you look to him, he will give you the right perspective. He will equip you to handle whatever comes your way, and he will remind you of his strength and power. With God on your side, you have nothing to worry about.

Trustworthy One, there is no one like you. You are faithful, strong, and wise. You see everything clearly; nothing is a mystery to you. I trust you with my life.

IN EVERYTHING

Seek his will in all you do,
and he will show you which path to take.

PROVERBS 3:6 NLT

God does not withhold his wisdom from those who seek it. He doesn't hide so that no one can find him. He is close, and he is easy to please. He eagerly shares the riches of his kingdom with you whenever you ask him. Don't insist on doing things your own way when God delights in sharing the abundance of his wisdom.

When you seek the Lord and have fellowship with his Spirit, you will be able to follow his leadership more readily. The more you get to know him, the more familiar you will be with his voice. Remain humble and open to his direction, and he will steer you down the right path.

Lord, I trust you to show me which way to go and which decisions to make. Even when your voice is not loud, I know that I can trust your character. I love you.

LIGHT OF LIFE

"I am the Light of the world; the one who follows Me will not walk in the darkness, but will have the Light of life."

JOHN 8:12 NASB

The promise of the Light of life is the promise of Jesus' presence wherever you go. He is the one who provides you with light and hope. He is the reason you can see clearly even though the world is dark all around you. He is pure light and life, and in him you are fully alive.

Seeing clearly doesn't mean that you understand every situation you come across. It doesn't mean that you have the answers to everyone's questions or that you aren't affected by the injustice or suffering in the world. You see clearly because you have a personal relationship with the author and perfecter of your faith. You are not shaken because you know that God is in control and the love of Christ will prevail.

Light of the World, I look to you today for understanding, hope, and direction. You are the one who fills me up when I am empty. I need you, Lord. Shine on me.

CONSTANT PEACE

He himself is our peace, who has made us both one and has broken down in his flesh the dividing wall of hostility.

EPHESIANS 2:14 ESV

In a world filled with chaos, uncertainty, and hostility, where do you find peace? Though you may long for peace in this world, there is a true and lasting peace available even now in the presence of God. His peace does not change with the shifting circumstances of the world.

As you spend time with God today, allow him to strengthen you in his presence. Allow him to give you his peace and equip you to face the world. Walk away from your deliberate time with him knowing that you can carry his peace with you everywhere you go. He has given you everything you need to go about your day with your heart at rest.

Prince of Peace, there is nothing that can keep me from your great love. Thank you for the palpable peace I find in your presence. I am yours, and I trust you.

GIVE CREDIT

We love because he first loved us.

1 JOHN 4:19 CSB

You can love others because God loves you. Every good, kind, or thoughtful thing you do comes from him. He is your source and your reason. He is your standard and your foundation. When you lay your life down for others in big and small ways, you reflect God's love to the world.

Give God the credit he is due. As you love others, recognize that he is the one who has equipped you to do it. When you are lacking in love, run to him and allow him to fill you up. Ask him for a greater understanding of his love, and he will give it to you.

Lord, I know that I have no reason to excuse my lack of love today. I come to you to be filled up. Holy Spirit, wash over me with the empowering grace of your presence.

WHATEVER YOU DO

Whether you eat or drink, or whatever you do, do all to the glory of God.

1 Corinthians 10:31 NKJV

Everything you do can reflect the mercy of Christ. You get to live out his love in your life, aligning with the fruit of his kingdom and the truth of his nature. When you are intentional about your actions, big or small, the thread of God's glorious grace is woven through your life.

How can you focus on glorifying God through your choices today? Everything you do is an opportunity to worship the Lord. How you start your morning and your conversations with your coworkers can glorify God. As you put the preferences of others first, you reflect the thoughtfulness of Christ. As you seek to be excellent in all you do, you reflect the excellence of God. Whatever you do, do it unto the Lord.

Lord, I want to be a true reflection of your love. Give me grace to commit everything I do to you. May my thoughts, words, and actions be glorifying to you.

RESTORED IN FULL

God is satisfied to have all his fullness dwelling in Christ. And by the blood of his cross, everything in heaven and earth is brought back to himself—back to its original intent, restored to innocence again!

COLOSSIANS 1:19-20 TPT

Christ is the fullness of God in human form. When you look at the life, ministry, and teachings of Christ, you can know that they are straight from the heart of God the Father. Therefore, everything he taught you to prioritize is what God wants you to prioritize.

Christ's sacrifice is the power of redemption not only for you but for everything in creation. You are restored to innocence in the powerful love of Christ. What he has done can never be undone, and the threats of darkness cannot overcome the redemptive power of his resurrection life. Find your hope and comfort in him. Trust him to continuously restore you in his presence.

Redeemer, thank you for the power of your restorative mercy that fills my life. Thank you for saving me and setting me free. Draw me closer to you and transform me in your presence.

SEEK AND FIND

"You will call on me and come and pray to me,
and I will listen to you.
You will seek me and find me
when you seek me with all your heart."

JEREMIAH 29:12-13 NIV

You will make time for the things you value. You will make room in your life for the things you want. If you want to be with God, make space for him. If you want your life to reflect his love, prioritize your relationship with him. He promises that you will not be disappointed.

Love the Lord with everything you have, and he will not leave you empty handed. If you seek him, you will find him. If you turn your heart toward him, you will be satisfied. When you ask for more of his presence, his response is guaranteed. Give your whole self to him and expect him to meet you.

Father, I will pray to you every time I think of you today. In every question, every challenge, and every joy, I will turn my attention to you. Reveal yourself to me as I do. Thank you.

COMPASSIONATE SAVIOR

When the Lord saw her, his heart overflowed with compassion. "Don't cry!" he said.

LUKE 7:13 NLT

In this passage of Scripture, Jesus came upon the funeral of a young man. When Jesus saw the grieving mother, he was moved with compassion. He went over to the coffin and told the boy to get up. Jesus restored a brokenhearted woman's hope by giving her back her son.

The Lord sees you in your grief, and he is moved with compassion to comfort you. He not only sees your pain, but he moves on your behalf. He has not forgotten you, and he does not overlook your tears. He doesn't ignore your wounds when you put them in his hands. He is a patient and skilled healer. Trust him with your hurt, and he will transform it into something beautiful.

Restorer, I want to know the power of your compassion at work in my life and the lives of those around me. Restore the parts of my heart that are broken. I trust you with my pain.

DAILY SURRENDER

I am confident of this very thing, that he who began a good work among you will complete it by the day of Christ Jesus.

PHILIPPIANS 1:6 NASB

You are not a lost cause. The parts of your life that never seem to change are not hopeless. Keep in my mind that you have no idea how and when God will move. Just because you haven't seen healing in certain areas doesn't mean it isn't going to happen. It can be hard to maintain faith, but the good news is that even your faith is sustained by the grace of God.

Submit your life to God on a daily basis. Turn toward him in surrender as often as it comes to mind and trust that he will faithfully transform your life. Allow his love to work in your life however he deems. He knows exactly what you need and when you need it. Put your ideas of progress into his hands and allow him to complete his work in your life according to his good and perfect will.

Faithful One, thank you for your persistent mercy. I trust you to finish your work in my life. Give me confidence in your ability when I am overwhelmed or discouraged by my progress.

LOOK FOR THE FRUIT

The fruit of the Spirit is love, joy, peace, patience, kindness, goodness, faithfulness, gentleness, self-control; against such things there is no law.

GALATIANS 5:22-23 ESV

It is helpful to know what the fruit of God's kingdom looks, feels, and tastes like. Otherwise, you'll feel tossed about by every trial or obstacle that comes your way. The fruit of the Spirit is like a compass. It shows you which direction to go, and it keeps you from being lost.

God is present wherever you see the fruit of the Spirit. If your actions do not produce the fruit of the Spirit, you can assume that something isn't lining up. When you submit to the Lord and adopt his ways as your own, there will be tangible evidence in your life. Look for the presence of his fruit and thank him for his work in your heart.

Spirit, thank you for sowing seeds of peace, goodness, and joy. The characteristics of how you move are clear to me. Though I cannot always pin you down, I see your fruit and am in awe of what you do.

HE CARRIES YOU

For the joy that lay before him, he endured the cross, despising the shame, and sat down at the right hand of the throne of God.

HEBREWS 12:2 CSB

Jesus is the best example to follow for living humbly, openly, and compassionately. He endured whatever came his way while keeping his attention fixed on the end goal. His eyes were trained on the Father no matter what happened. He was constantly prioritizing the connection he had with God.

How can you live through difficult seasons? Keep your eyes on the Father. How can you persevere when you don't have any strength left? Remember the source of your hope. Nothing on this earth lasts forever. Every single trial you face will pass. Cling to Jesus and he will carry you through.

Loving Lord, I raise my gaze above the temporary troubles and trials of this life to the eternal glory of your kingdom. You are full of love, and you won't ever keep it from me. Thank you.

CONSTANT COMPANION

"Very truly I tell you, it is for your good that I am going away. Unless I go away, the Advocate will not come to you; but if I go, I will send him to you."

JOHN 16:7 NIV

Jesus did not abandon humanity when he ascended to heaven after his resurrection. He gave the gift of the Holy Spirit. He actually said that it's better to have the Holy Spirit than to have himself. Jesus is one man, but the Holy Spirit is not bound by physical limitations. He offers comfort, support, and guidance to every believer simultaneously.

If you are unfamiliar with the person and the work of the Holy Spirit, spend some time getting to know him. Read through Scripture and pay close attention to any mention of the Spirit. Notice how he moves and become familiar with his character. As you do, you'll see what an incredible gift it is to have his constant companionship.

Jesus Christ, thank you for the gift of the Holy Spirit. Thank you for giving me an advocate, teacher, and friend who is always with me.

WORKS THAT SHINE

"Let your light so shine before men, that they may see your good works and glorify your Father in heaven."

MATTHEW 5:16 NKJV

How you treat others, the choices you make, and the attitudes you adopt reveal the values of your heart. If you belong to Christ and follow his ways, then your actions will reflect it. As you experience God's grace, you are empowered to extend it to others. As you are transformed by his love, you can share his love with the people around you.

Everything you do toward others is meant to be extension of the way God has treated you. If you are struggling to be merciful to others, ask God to give you a revelation of his mercy toward you. If you have a hard time being patient, ask God to remind you of his patience toward you. Every area of personal weakness is an opportunity for you to gain a deeper understanding of God's love for you.

Holy God, it is because of who you are that I am who I am. Thank you for your mercy, patience, and grace. Help me to never withhold from others what you freely offer me.

MAY

Don't worry about anything, but in everything,
through prayer and petition with thanksgiving,
present your requests to God.

Philippians 4:6 CSB

TRUSTWORTHY ONES

You can't trust a gossiper with a secret;
they'll just go blab it all.
Put your confidence instead in a trusted friend,
for he will be faithful to keep it in confidence.

Proverbs 11:13 TPT

You can't control the actions of other people. At some point or another you'll be disappointed by someone else's behavior. Sometimes disappointment happens when you share information with the wrong person. It can be disheartening to realize that you can't trust someone you thought you could.

Instead of focusing on the people who have hurt you, think about the people in your life who have remained steady. Even one friend who is reliable and kind is a sweet gift. Nurture the faithful friendships in your life and trust God with the hearts of people who have let you down.

Perfect One, I know that no one is perfect except you, but I am grateful for the true and steadfast ones in my life. I'm so grateful for trusted friends. May each of my relationships be honoring to you.

HOPEFUL PLANS

"For I know the plans I have for you," declares the LORD, "plans to prosper you and not to harm you, plans to give you hope and a future."

JEREMIAH 29:11 NIV

It can be unnerving to navigate a path you've never traveled on. It's normal to try to hold on to control especially when you're unsure of what might happen. When you don't know what tomorrow will bring, it can be helpful to ground yourself in the faithfulness of the Lord.

When you are anxious, God is calm. When you are troubled, he is steady. He sees every possibility and guides you with his strong right hand. He will not lead you astray, and he does not expect you to figure everything out on your own. In all circumstances, his presence is your source of peace and hope.

Lord, I'm so glad you know what is ahead, even when I have no idea. I trust you to guide me in your love and to keep my heart preserved in your peace. I look to you.

IN EVERY SITUATION

I know how to live on almost nothing or with everything. I have learned the secret of living in every situation, whether it is with a full stomach or empty, with plenty or little. For I can do everything through Christ, who gives me strength.

PHILIPPIANS 4:12-13 NLT

No matter how much control you think you have, you cannot escape the reality of life. Difficult things will happen. Pain and suffering are inevitable. If you base God's faithfulness on the circumstances of your life, you will be disappointed. Instead, focus on his promise to be present with you through every trial you face.

The secret to enduring the ups and downs of life is to remain connected to Jesus Christ. His presence offers grace, strength, and hope despite your circumstances. No matter what your life looks like, he remains steady and unchanging.

Faithful One, thank you for the fellowship I have with your Spirit in every moment. You are my source of strength and my hope. I rely on you.

GREATER STILL

You have been a stronghold for the helpless,
A stronghold for the poor in his distress,
A refuge from the storm, a shade from the heat;
For the breath of the ruthless
Is like a rain storm against a wall.

Isaiah 25:4 NASB

God is a defense for the helpless and a refuge for the needy. He protects the oppressed, and he does not overlook the weary. He is strong in the face of injustice, and he promises to intervene on behalf of the vulnerable.

When you are weak, without anyone to come to your rescue, the Lord is near. Look to him, call out to him, and lean on him. He is closer than you realize. In his presence, he offers you everything you need. Though your trials might be great, God's ability to lead you through them is greater.

Mighty God, there is no one like you in all the earth. You are the only one who can truly help me when I am helpless. I turn to you and trust you to be my refuge.

HEAVENLY TREASURES

We have not received the spirit of the world, but the Spirit who comes from God, so that we may understand what has been freely given to us by God.

1 Corinthians 2:12 CSB

God is unimpressed by shows of power and prestige. His standard of success is entirely different from the world's. His kingdom is defined by different principles, and he values everything the world says is worthless.

When you follow God, you'll stand out from the world. Instead of being motivated by prestige, power, and monetary gain, your life will be an active reflection of God's mercy, peace, love, and hope. As you lean on the Spirit in all things and accept God's generous gift of grace, you will find that the treasures of the world will fade away.

Lord, deepen my understanding of your character and continue to lead me in your powerful mercy. I choose to follow your ways over the systems of this world. Help me gather heavenly treasures rather than worldly ones.

UPLIFTING ENCOURAGEMENT

Encourage one another and build one another up, just as you are doing.

1 THESSALONIANS 5:11 ESV

Have you ever longed for encouragement? Have you ever felt alone and overlooked? Through those experiences you know that a kind word at the right time can be priceless. A deliberate word of encouragement can be the difference between despair and perseverance.

When your heart becomes discouraged, let those feelings motivate you to lift up the people around you. There is true satisfaction found in laying your life down for others. Instead of wallowing or feeling sorry for yourself, remember that in Christ you are fully equipped. He has lavished his love on you and given you everything you need to love others.

Father, give me grace to encourage others. Give me a loving attitude and the right words to say. Help me lay my life down in an effort to lift others up.

REST ON EVERY SIDE

"Is not the LORD your God with you? And has He not given you rest on every side? For He has given the inhabitants of the land into my hand, and the land is subdued before the LORD and before His people."

1 CHRONICLES 22:18 NKJV

God's presence brings peace to your mind, heart, and body. No matter what today holds, the Lord is with you. When you begin to worry, turn your attention to the nearness of his presence. He is not far away; he is as close as your breath.

Let the peace of God put your heart at ease. Give him your burdens and allow him to take care of you. You are his child, and he loves being your Father. There is no reason to be overcome with worry when God offers you rest.

Good Shepherd, thank you for the rest you offer me in the midst of tempests and trials. Your presence brings peace, and I find restoration in you. Thank you.

BLESSED TO SERVE

Does your life in Christ give you strength? Does his love comfort you? Do we share together in the spirit? Do you have mercy and kindness? If so, make me very happy by having the same thoughts, sharing the same love, and having one mind and purpose.

PHILIPPIANS 2:1-2 NCV

The beauty and strength you find in fellowship with the Lord is not meant for you alone. It is a gift to offer to others. You are meant to share with the people around you and encourage each other to lay your lives down for the Lord. You were created to live in unity with a community of people.

Whether you open your homes to others, offer a helping hand to someone in need, or comfort those who are grieving, you are partnering with Jesus. His life within you spurs you on to embrace a servant-hearted lifestyle. You are blessed when you put the needs of others before your own.

Generous One, there is no one more benevolent, thoughtful, and kind than you are. I want to be more like you, so I will choose to partner with your goodness as I look for ways to share with others today.

EMPOWERED TO LOVE

God will never give you the spirit of fear, but the Holy Spirit who gives you mighty power, love, and self-control.

2 Timothy 1:7 TPT

God does not lead with fear. He does not push or prod you in order to keep you in line. He does not hold an impossible standard over your head, and he does not use intimidation to get you to change your ways. He leads with love in every way. He uses kindness to encourage you to lay your life down.

As you spend time with the Lord soaking up his love, he will empower you to love others in the same way. If you allow him to, he will give you grace to treat people with a level of kindness that is beyond your own ability. He empowers you to love others with a selfless, gracious, and merciful attitude.

Gracious God, there isn't a day where you put aside your mercy or love. I want to be more like you. Give me grace to selflessly love those around me.

NOT CRUSHED

We are hard pressed on every side, but not crushed; perplexed, but not in despair.

2 CORINTHIANS 4:8 NIV

When life brings unavoidable hurdles your way, you are not doomed. Though you may be cast down, you will not be overcome. Even when your situation seems hopeless and you are unsure of how it could possibly work out, God is in control. He is your Prince of Peace, Defender, and Savior.

Do you feel crushed today? Do the pressures of life feel like they are too much to bear? When nothing makes sense and you cannot take another step, Jesus is your hope. Allow him to comfort you in your distress. Look to him for guidance and encouragement.

Jesus Christ, I trust that I will not be crushed by the pressures that seem to be building around me. You are my peace, hope, and strength. I trust in you. Be glorified in my life.

STEP BY STEP

Let your roots grow down into him, and let your lives be built on him. Then your faith will grow strong in the truth you were taught, and you will overflow with thankfulness.

Colossians 2:7 NLT

If you want to grow strong in faith, you must remain rooted in the mercy of Christ. Allow your roots to grow deep in his love. This is done by getting to know him, digging deep into his Word, and spending time with him in prayer. Your yielded heart makes room for Christ to come in and do a marvelous work.

Gaining strength takes time. Your relationship with God probably looks different now than it did years ago, and it will look even more different in the years to come. You aren't expected to have everything figured out right now. A life built on Jesus does not happen overnight and there aren't steps that can be skipped. Give yourself the grace to quietly follow him, trusting that he knows how to lead you.

Wise God, thank you for the power of your wisdom at work in my life. I trust you as my God, my shepherd, and my teacher.

STONE TO FLESH

"I will give them one heart, and put a new spirit within them. And I will remove the heart of stone from their flesh and give them a heart of flesh."

EZEKIEL 11:19 NASB

God is an expert at changing hearts. He is the only one who can take the hardness of your heart and soften it. His mercy transforms you from the inside out. His ability to turn stone to flesh should give you an incredible amount of hope.

You are no longer a slave to your own weaknesses. You are not bound to negativity or destruction. When you can't muster up the ability to change, God can intervene. When you can't figure out how to move forward, God can move on your behalf. It delights him to give you new life.

Merciful God, I put my heart in your hands. You are the only one who can transform me from the inside out. I trust you to do what I cannot.

AGELESS GRACE

"I will pour out my Spirit on all humanity;
then your sons and your daughters will prophesy,
your old men will have dreams,
and your young men will see visions."

Joel 2:28 CSB

Both the young and old have a place in the kingdom of God. No one is disqualified from being used by the Spirit of God. If you feel behind in life or past your prime, know that there is no such thing in Christ's kingdom.

You have a purpose and a place in Christ. Your age or experience does not exclude you. God has poured out his Spirit on all flesh, and that includes yours. He offers you gifts that are yours to practice and put to use. He is not stingy with his goodness or kindness. You have more than you can imagine in the fellowship of his Spirit.

Holy Spirit, thank you for reaching me as I am, and for depositing elements of Christ's kingdom into my heart and life. I am in awe of you, and I am humbled by your nearness. I am open, Lord, pour out a fresh portion of your presence today.

NEVER TURNED AWAY

"All that the Father gives me will come to me, and whoever comes to me I will never cast out."

JOHN 6:37 ESV

Christ never turns away those who come to him. He embraces you with love, and he keeps you firmly rooted in his mercy. He does not cast you away, and he will never lose sight of you. He is a good shepherd and faithful friend.

Lay aside your worries of not getting it right today no matter what "it" is. Christ doesn't need your perfection; he just wants your willingness. Come to him and don't delay. You are always met with kindness when you do. Let the power of God's love wash over you as you turn toward him. He is good, and in him you have a forever home.

King Jesus, I'm so grateful that I can't lose my place in your kingdom. Your love is stronger than death, and it is more powerful than my mistakes. You are forever good, and I won't stop looking to you.

HE DIRECTS

A man's heart plans his way,
But the Lord directs his steps.

Proverbs 16:9 NKJV

It is good to make plans for tomorrow and to take steps toward your goals. However, it is important to know that your plans won't be perfect. You can't anticipate what you don't know, and the future always holds some element of mystery.

The Lord, in his goodness, sees everything clearly. Nothing can surprise him. Even when it looks like your plans are falling apart, God is able to direct you. Though you may experience disappointment as you let go of what you thought would be seamless, God was never under the impression that it would be perfect. He is able to guide you in wisdom for he is trustworthy, faithful, and true.

Yahweh, you always account for what I can't see, and for that I am grateful. I give up needing to know every detail of my future and trust you to direct my steps.

COURAGE TO CONQUER

On the day I called you, you answered me.
You made me strong and brave.

Psalm 138:3 NCV

God is your ready help whenever you call on him. You don't have to wait for the right time to reach out to him. Whenever you reach out to him it is always the right time. He is faithful and true, and he always comes through. He offers strength for your weakness and courage for your fear. He is so very good, and he is always ready to respond to you.

Though you may be caught off guard by the troubles of life, God is not. He is able to do far more than you can think of asking. He does not grow weary of you asking for his help. His grace is abundant, and his mercy is never-ending. With that kind of supply, you need never limit your requests for his help.

Victorious One, give me grace to look to you every time I feel fear closing in on me. You are so good, and I don't want to limit what you don't limit.

LET GOD HELP

Put your heart and soul into every activity you do, as though you are doing it for the Lord himself and not merely for others.

COLOSSIANS 3:23 TPT

When you work tirelessly for others, you can reach a point of burnout. Clues that you have reached this point include bitterness at others for asking for help, general exhaustion around work and relationships, as well as a lack of desire to engage in activities you normally love. This is not how God wants you to live.

God's desire is for you to love others out of the overflow of his love. This is not meant to be burdensome or based on your own strength. He is the one who asks you to love others, and he is the one who equips you to do it. Let yourself off the hook and trust him to do what you cannot.

Lord, pour your love into my heart. Give me what I need to love others as you love them. Thank you for equipping me to live according to your calling.

DON'T WORRY

"Do not worry about your life, what you will eat or drink; or about your body, what you will wear. Is not life more than food, and the body more than clothes? Look at the birds of the air; they do not sow or reap or store away in barns, and yet your heavenly Father feeds them. Are you not much more valuable than they? Can any one of you by worrying add a single hour to your life?"

MATTHEW 6:25-27 NIV

God knows your heart. He sees each of your worries and fears. He doesn't make light of your concerns or belittle you for being afraid, but he does call you to be unhindered by worry. He empowers you with his grace to be free in his love. He takes care of you and gives you peace when you ask for it.

Instead of letting worry weigh you down, you can trust God to take care of what you cannot control. Knowing that you can't add value to your life by worry, you will experience relief as you choose to trust the Lord. Then you can redirect that energy to something more fruitful and life-giving.

Jesus, thank you for the reminder that worry is wasted energy. I trust you to take care of what I cannot.

OPPORTUNITIES FOR JOY

When troubles of any kind come your way, consider it an opportunity for great joy. For you know that when your faith is tested, your endurance has a chance to grow.

JAMES 1:2-3 NLT

Every test and challenge are an opportunity for greater joy. Though the trials of life bring discomfort, pain, and change, they cannot steal the gifts God has given you. When unexpected challenges arise, you can shift your perspective from frustration to confident expectation. No matter what you go through, God is the same good God. He still offers you everything you need, and he promises to never leave you.

Looking for the silver lining doesn't mean ignoring the realities of life. You can remain hopeful while also accepting what comes your way. You don't have to dwell in despair. You can walk through grief and still know that there is more joy to experience. Every trial is an opportunity for growth.

Lord, I want to know your joy even in disappointment. Help me to look at the troubles of life as opportunities for growth, greater joy, and deeper understanding of who you are.

READY TO HELP

The Lord God helps me,
Therefore, I am not disgraced;
Therefore, I have made my face like flint,
And I know that I will not be ashamed.

Isaiah 50:7 NASB

Holy determination is yours when you are convinced of God's help. When his Spirit empowers you to keep going, even when everything feels as if it is falling apart, you can stand strong and persevere in faith. You don't have to conjure up your own strength when God is ready and able to help you.

As you spend time with God, he will equip you for the day ahead. He knows exactly what each moment of your life will look like, and he is fully capable of providing for you. When you rely on him through the hardest parts of life, you strengthen your faith and cultivate resolve in your spirit.

Lord God, I believe that you are my help and that the power of your mercy and grace is available even now. Help me rise up in courage and to keep persevering in your love even when it's hard. I need you, and I trust you.

CONTENTMENT IS POWERFUL

Keep your lives free from the love of money. Be satisfied with what you have; for he himself has said, "I will never leave you or abandon you."

HEBREWS 13:5 CSB

Consumerism runs rampant in society. Though you may have all you need at the moment, it is difficult to maintain peace when you are constantly being told you don't have enough. Though the pull for consumption is real, the satisfaction it offers is temporary.

Choose gratitude every time you feel yourself being pulled toward wanting what is advertised to you today. Intentionally think about your blessings when you feel pangs of envy or comparison. Keep a running list of reasons to be thankful. Let each big or small item nurture contentment and gratitude in your heart.

Lord, I don't want to mindlessly consume everything that is offered to me. Help me cultivate self-control and contentment. Give me grace to say no to comparison or jealousy. Fill me with gratitude for the many blessings you've given me.

REACHING FOR APPROVAL

Am I now seeking the approval of man, or of God? Or am I trying to please man? If I were still trying to please man, I would not be a servant of Christ.

Galatians 1:10 ESV

When you are reaching for the approval of others, you will constantly shift yourself to fit the image of what they find acceptable. It is a losing battle with a moving target. Instead of trying to fit in with others, what would it look like to be grounded in your identity in Christ and look to please God?

Be honest with yourself today. Whose approval are you really looking for? Don't beat yourself up for wanting to please others if that's what is there. Thank God for the ability to redirect and choose differently today. Remember that God's expectations are not difficult to meet. His burden is light, and his yoke is easy.

Worthy Lord, thank you for the patience you have with me. I don't want to wake up one day and realize I wasted my life on what others wanted for me. I want to live in the freedom of your love and please you above all else.

BUILT OTHERS UP

Let no corrupt word proceed out of your mouth, but what is good for necessary edification, that it may impart grace to the hearers.

Ephesians 4:29 NKJV

Careless speech hinders relationships from flourishing. You can build others up with your words, and you can also inflict harm. You don't need to expect perfection from yourself, but you can certainly take steps toward being more mindful. Humbly take responsibility for the words that you speak.

When you realize that you have hurt others with your words, be quick to reconcile and offer a sincere apology. It can be uncomfortable to admit you are wrong, but it will strengthen your relationships. Vulnerability and teachability produce intimacy. Approaching your mistakes with humility leaves room for growth.

Gracious God, thank you for the limitless grace I find in your presence. You are always better than I expected. Give me grace to change when I find myself tearing others down instead of building them up.

DO WHAT YOU LOVE

They do not worry about how short life is,
because God keeps them busy with what they love to do.

ECCLESIASTES 5:20 NCV

Following God is not meant to be burdensome or overwhelming. Don't buy into the faulty assumption that God wants everything you do to be a painful sacrifice. You honor him when you use the gifts he's given you with joy. He might push you out of your comfort zone at times, but he isn't plotting how to make you miserable.

Doing what you love delights God. Using your natural talents in his name is an act of worship. He loves it when you use the gifts he's given you. Today, think about what cultivates feelings of fulfillment and offer it to God with thanksgiving.

Lord, I want my life to be a blessing to you. Show me the gifts and talents you've given me. Empower me to practice them unto your glory. Thank you for the way you made me.

NOTHING WASTED

We are convinced that every detail of our lives is continually woven together for good, for we are his lovers who have been called to fulfill his designed purpose.

ROMANS 8:28 TPT

Every detail of your life is woven together by the Lord. He uses even what seems completely wasted to bring restoration, redemption, and hope. As you follow him, he orchestrates your days and empowers you to fulfill the purpose he's laid out for you.

Instead of dwelling in regret and shame, rise up in humble gratitude, knowing nothing is wasted in God's hands. He loves you to life over and over again. By his mercy and grace, even your mistakes can be used to create fruit in your life. He makes beauty out of ashes, and he creates new life out of everything he touches.

Good Father, I'm so grateful that you weave your gracious goodness through my life, bringing redemption and restoration. May I be a conduit of your mercy right where I am planted. I love you.

FIRM PLANS

The plans of the Lord stand firm forever,
the purposes of his heart through all generations.

Psalm 33:11 NIV

God's plans don't change even when yours do. You can trust his leadership because he sees everything perfectly. While you might be discouraged by the shifting of your path, God remains steady and unshaken. His ways are always best even when they don't look how you want.

While you can't possibly see the entire picture of your life, God doesn't miss a single detail. You can trust his perspective far more than your own. If you feel anxious about the direction of your life, lay your worries at his feet and confidently expect him to show you the way.

Faithful One, I trust that your plans are better than anyone else's including my own. You aren't surprised by what surprises me, and for that I am eternally grateful. I trust you to continue to lead me in wisdom, truth, and love.

HE WORKS WITHIN

God is working in you, giving you the desire and the power to do what pleases him.

PHILIPPIANS 2:13 NLT

You cannot work to please God. Your ability to honor him comes directly from him. He is the one who works in and through your life. This means that you can take a deep breath and surrender! Let go of your need for control and give up your tendency to strive for perfection.

Your responsibility is to respond to what God is already doing. As you remain humble and teachable, he transforms your heart into his likeness. As you stay soft hearted toward his instructions, he empowers you to walk in his ways. In all things, God is the one who teaches, leads, and directs you.

Merciful God, I open my heart to you today. I ask you to transform me. Thank you for working in my life and intervening on my behalf. Give me grace to respond to your leadership.

NEVER FORGOTTEN

"Are five sparrows not sold for two assaria? And yet not one of them has gone unnoticed in the sight of God."

LUKE 12:6 NASB

Take courage from the Word of the Lord when you feel overlooked. Find strength in the truth when you mourn the suffering of others. No one is forgotten by God. If he cares for the birds of the air, how much more will he care for you?

God sees you. He is aware of every tiny detail of your life. He notices when you are hurt, and he grieves alongside you when you suffer. He celebrates your victories, and he is proud of your efforts. As you spend time with him today, be affirmed that your good Father has not forgotten you.

Lord, thank you for your watchful eye over my life. Thank you for your kindness and attentiveness toward me and each of your children. Help me remember how valuable I am to you.

SUSTAINED

He found him in a desolate land,
in a barren, howling wilderness;
he surrounded him, cared for him,
and protected him as the pupil of his eye.

DEUTERONOMY 32:10 CSB

When you feel like you are walking in the wilderness, you are not alone. Even in the harshest spiritual climates and the most desolate places, God sustains, shields, and cares for you. If you look to the Lord, he will never abandon you.

May you find your hope in the presence of God. May you feel strengthened from the inside out as you turn your eyes toward him. May you experience the comfort of his love and the security of his provision. No matter what your circumstances look like, he is with you.

Faithful God, I don't want to live under the illusion that life is meant to be easy. I want to know your peace in the chaos and your closeness in the wilderness. Be near, oh God, and sustain me.

PERVASIVE PEACE

"I have said these things to you, that in me you may have peace. In the world you will have tribulation. But take heart; I have overcome the world."

John 16:33 ESV

The peace that Christ offers you is not dependent upon the circumstances of life. Scripture warns that you will suffer in this world. God didn't want any of his followers to be taken by surprise when it happened. Christ, your living hope, has overcome the world. He overcame death when he resurrected from the grave. In him, you have peace that passes all understanding.

What are the things that upset the peace of your heart? When troubles come, do you find yourself prone to questioning whether God is truly good? Offer your anxieties to the Lord. His Spirit is near, and he is able to calm your anxious thoughts.

Prince of Peace, thank you for the power of your peace. Flood me with your peace today and settle my heart in your presence.

SACRIFICE OF PRAISE

By him let us continually offer the sacrifice of praise to God, that is, the fruit of our lips, giving thanks to his name.

HEBREWS 13:15 NKJV

Through Christ, you can offer a continual sacrifice of praise to God. You look ahead with hope, knowing his kingdom is your true home. In the meantime, this life is what you have to offer him. Every messy, imperfect, beautiful moment is yours to surrender to him.

Worshipping God is simpler than you might think. It doesn't have to be a production or a complicated process. Praising God is as simple as turning your eyes toward him no matter what your circumstances are. You can honor him with every breath, tear, cry of anguish, or burst of laughter.

Worthy One, I look past the inconveniences of today and choose to offer you my heart. Forgive me for complicating my worship of you. I praise you because you are worthy, and you never change. Receive my sacrifice of praise.

JUNE

Those who trust in the Lord
will renew their strength;
they will soar like eagles;
they will run and not become weary,
they will walk and not faint.

Isaiah 40:31 csb

ALWAYS FAITHFUL

If we are not faithful, he will still be faithful,
because he must be true to who he is.

2 Timothy 2:13 NCV

Even when you fail miserably, God does not change his ways. His nature is as merciful, faithful, and true as it has been or ever will be. God's faithfulness does not depend on your faithfulness. This is why you can readily bring him your failures. No matter what you present him with, his character remains the same.

God's presence is a safe place. When you run to him for some quiet time, don't be afraid to bare your soul. There is no reason to fear his reaction. Enter his presence with an armful of burdens but walk away with a light heart. Lean fully on the steadiness of God.

Great God, I'm so grateful that your faithfulness is not dependent upon my own. You are so much better than I give you credit for, and your love is so much bigger than I can fathom.

HOPE AND STRENGTH

Things never discovered or heard of before, things beyond our ability to imagine—these are the many things God has in store for all his lovers.

1 Corinthians 2:9 TPT

Spend time today dreaming about the goodness of God and what it looks like. He has better things in store for you than anything you've experienced or could imagine. All the good things you could think of fall short of the glory of his love.

Hoping in God's goodness doesn't mean ignoring the reality of your life. He is not asking you to be unrealistically positive. He's asking you to recognize that the best is yet to come. He knows that life can be painful, but he offers you strength that comes from knowing it won't last forever.

Good God, as I imagine your goodness, broaden my perspective of hope. Let expectation and joy arise as I fix my heart on you. You are incomparably good, and I continue to trust you with my life.

EVERLASTING GOD

"The Lord is the everlasting God,
the Creator of the ends of the earth.
He will not grow tired or weary,
and his understanding no one can fathom."

Isaiah 40:28 NIV

It is almost too much to comprehend that God is everlasting. He existed before the beginning of time, and he will continue to exist after everything you know has faded away. He is the source of all life. Everything finds its wholeness in him.

This God who was, is, and is yet to come is the one who watches over you. He does not grow tired or weary. His understanding is far greater than your own. May you trust him, follow him, and draw your strength from him. He will carry you through each of your days, for he is faithful and true.

Everlasting One, when I am feeling overwhelmed by life, I will remember the truth that you are never overwhelmed. You don't get tired of acting out of love. You don't grow weary. I trust you, Lord.

GOOD SHEPHERD

"If a man has a hundred sheep and one of them gets lost, what will he do? Won't he leave the ninety-nine others in the wilderness and go to search for the one that is lost until he finds it?"

LUKE 15:4 NLT

God always goes after a lost sheep. Heaven and earth rejoice at the redemption of one lost lamb. No matter how far you wander, you are never out of God's reach. There is no distance in existence that God cannot cross to find you.

If you have wandering away from God, it is never too late to turn around and be swept up by his love. He rejoices over you as his own, and he will not shame you. He is so much better than anyone you've ever known. Receive the grace, redemption, and love he pursues you with today.

Good Shepherd, I want to be wrapped up in the embrace of your loving care. Draw me back to you and remind me of your goodness. You are so kind, patient, and powerful. I love you.

SPIRIT INTERCESSION

The Spirit also helps our weakness; for we do not know what to pray for as we should, but the Spirit Himself intercedes for us with groanings too deep for words.

Romans 8:26 NASB

You are not powerless when you are at a loss for how to pray. It is an opportunity for the Spirit to intervene and intercede on your behalf. You don't have to have the right words. The Spirit reads your heart and prays for you. Even in your prayer life, you aren't expected to rely on your own strength.

As you spend time with God today, surrender your need to be in control. Ask him to soften your heart and director your time with him. He will lead you where you need to go. He will mend what is broken and equip you to move forward according to his will. In all things, he is your faithful guide.

Holy Spirit, I invite you to read my heart when I have no understanding of my own feelings or how to pray. You know me through and through. Be my intercessor before the Father and pour out your grace, healing, and mercy upon me as I sit in your presence.

INNER STRENGTH

I pray that he may grant you, according to the riches of his glory, to be strengthened with power in your inner being through his Spirit.

EPHESIANS 3:16 CSB

Inner strength is not found in the resources you may or may not have. It is not determined by your social status, how much money you make, or the stability of your relationships. Inner strength can only be found in the riches of God's glory.

When you feel like you are coming up short, God's gracious Spirit will empower you. When you feel like everything is falling apart, you don't need to muster up the ability to overcome. Strength comes from relying on God and entrusting your circumstances to him. He is the one who gives you what you need, and he is the one who shares his goodness with you.

Spirit of God, fill me up according to your riches. When I am weak, be my strength. I want to know the incomparable goodness and strength of your Spirit working in me.

SHARE THE WEIGHT

Share each other's burdens,
and in this way obey the law of Christ.

GALATIANS 6:2 NLT

Through Christ you were brought into God's family. You have brothers and sisters who don't share any of your genetics. Your connection to other believers is founded upon and strengthened by the blood of Jesus. His death and resurrection are the great unifier.

As part of a family, you have people you can depend on. You can ask for help, advice, comfort, and strength when you need it. You can confess your sins and expect other believers to encourage you. In the same way, you can lift up the people around you. Love the believers around you as family and you will honor God. Treat them with kindness, display sacrificial love, and pursue unity.

Gracious God, I know that I wasn't created to carry the weight of burdens too heavy to bear. Show me how to share my own problems in healthy ways, while also looking for ways to help others with theirs.

HE SEES IT ALL

God is not unjust so as to overlook your work and the love that you have shown for his name in serving the saints, as you still do.

Hebrews 6:10 ESV

It can be discouraging to feel as though your work is overlooked. You might feel demotivated, hurt, or even angry. When feelings of entitlement and bitterness begin to creep in, it's a good time to invite the Lord to examine and soften your heart.

God sees everything you do. Even when other people don't notice your efforts, he is aware of you. If you are working unto him, you will be less likely to be offended when something goes unseen. Honestly ask yourself whose praise you are searching for and allow God to encourage you when you are frustrated. He will give you just the right rewards for your hard work.

God, I trust that you don't overlook any sacrifice I make in your name. I trust you to see, know, and remember everything I do. I know you won't let me down.

EACH STEP

You do not know what will happen tomorrow! Your life is like a mist. You can see it for a short time, but then it goes away.

JAMES 4:14 NCV

When you perpetually put off what matters until tomorrow, you may wake up to find that your time has run out. Every day is a gift, and it matters how you spend it. You cannot say what tomorrow will bring, but you can approach each moment with intentionality and flexibility.

When you intentionally offer God your time, he will help you make the most of it. When you are flexible toward change and unforeseen circumstances, you will continuously move forward with less stress. Rather than worrying about if you're doing enough, remember that God is capable of ordering each of your days. Trust his leadership and lean on him for each next step.

Lord, I believe that your goodness meets me in every moment. Help me to be steady when I want to procrastinate. Give me grace to make the most of each day I have.

NOURISHING LOVE

"I love each of you with the same love that the Father loves me. You must continually let my love nourish your hearts."

JOHN 15:9 TPT

Be nourished by God's love today. Feast upon it and let it fill you up until you are satisfied. When your soul is filled with longing, God's love is what you need. When you are tired and overwhelmed, his love builds up your strength. When you are frustrated and hurt, his love brings healing and softness.

In all things, God's love is what you need. No matter the state of your heart, his love is your provision and nourishment. Turn to him in every circumstance and stay connected to him through the Holy Spirit. Dwell on the goodness of his love and find satisfaction in his presence.

Loving Lord, your love is the source of my life, and I don't want to neglect its power. You are present in love at every moment, and I want to continually be filled.

NO MATTER WHAT

The LORD is good to those whose hope is in him,
to the one who seeks him.

LAMENTATIONS 3:25 NIV

When the storms of this world rage, it can be tempting to question where the goodness of God is in the midst of it. Instead of blaming God, what if you offered him your honest frustrations and doubts? He welcomes your questions. He knows the struggles you face, and he doesn't expect you to have the right attitude every moment of every day.

There is comfort in being honest with God because his character never changes. Even when you are shaken by the circumstances of the world, God remains steady. The solid bedrock of his nature is strong enough to hold the weight of your doubt. Put your hope in him and trust him to lead you no matter what. Don't give up seeking him even if you are struggling through your feelings. He is reliable even when you have questions.

Good God, there is no one like you. You are steadfast in love, and your goodness is sure. I trust you to lead me through the hills and the valleys of this life. Bolster my hope in your presence and give me your peace.

EXTRAVAGANCE

"He returned home to his father. And while he was still a long way off, his father saw him coming. Filled with love and compassion, he ran to his son, embraced him, and kissed him."

Luke 15:20 NLT

Take some time to read through the entire parable of the prodigal son. Look at the choices of the young son and the attitude of the father. Did the father's love ever waver? God is a good, good Father. As soon as you turn toward him, he comes running to meet you. He wraps you up in the garments of his mercy and erases your shame.

Wherever you find yourself today, know that the Father's love is fierce and unchanging. His compassion toward you is like a rushing river. Whether it's been one day or several years since you glanced his way, remember that he longs to run to you like a good father would. Believe him when he says he will never leave you or forsake you.

Good Father, thank you for not tempering your love. I want to come alive in the redemption of your complete compassion today. Cover me in your love and speak your truth over my identity.

POWERFUL WORD

The word of God is living and active, and sharper than any two-edged sword, even penetrating as far as the division of soul and spirit, of both joints and marrow, and able to judge the thoughts and intentions of the heart.

HEBREWS 4:12 NASB

God's Word is a wonderful gift. As you read it today, allow it to achieve God's purposes in your life. Don't shy away from encouragement or conviction. Let the truth of the Word grow deep roots in your heart and bear abundant fruit in your life.

The Word of God is dynamic. It doesn't matter how many times you've read it, there is always something new to be found. Don't let long-time habits reduce Scripture's poignancy in your life. Just because you might have read something several times doesn't mean it isn't just as powerful as if you've never seen it. Ask God for a fresh perspective and a renewed hunger for the Word.

Lord, move in my heart how only you can. Cut away the things that don't serve my good or your glory. Give me fresh eyes for your Word. May it bear fruit in my life as I read it.

LEARN TO LOVE

Do everything in love.

1 CORINTHIANS 16:14 CSB

If you want to live according to God's law of love, then you have to let go of the need to qualify who is deserving of it. You can't apply God's merciful love to your own actions while holding others to an unachievable standard. When you stop trying to change other people's lives or even opinions, you can let God's love do the work it's intended to do.

When you are tempted to lean on your own understanding or perspective, remember God's calling to do everything in love. Love does not insist on its own way or hold a record of wrongs. Love is patient, and love is kind. When your thoughts or actions don't align with that, ask God to transform your heart even further. He loves to teach his children to love.

Merciful God, help me to let go of every excuse I have to not show love to others. I can choose to be loving, even when I don't like someone. Thank you for that truth and help me live it out well.

NOT A MYSTERY

He has told you, O man, what is good:
and what does the LORD require of you
but to do justice, and to love kindness,
and to walk humbly with your God?

MICAH 6:8 ESV

Scripture doesn't hide God's will. It's not difficult to understand what he wants you to do. You are called to do justice, love kindness, and walk humbly before God. The way that is personified might be different for everyone, but the standard is the same. If your actions fall into those categories, you are following God's will.

The title of your job or the city you live in matter significantly less than whether or not your actions display the love of God. He cares more about your heart than the way you define your life. His expectations of you are not burdensome, and his will is not a mystery you must solve.

Wise One, thank you for making your will known. Give me grace to follow your instructions. May everything I do be defined by humility, kindness, and a love for justice.

HUMBLING PERSPECTIVE

When I consider Your heavens, the work of Your fingers,
The moon and the stars, which You have ordained,
What is man that You are mindful of him,
And the son of man that You visit him?

PSALM 8:3-4 NKJV

When was the last time you stood outside on a dark, clear night and simply gazed at the stars above? The longer you look, the more stars you can see. The more you see, the smaller your little world seems.

Consider the heavens and the creative work of God's hands. Allow the awe of creation to lead you to a perspective shift. While your life might seem insignificant compared to the vastness of the heavens, you are completely seen, known, and loved. Creation is a tapestry of God's glory, yet you are his masterpiece.

Creator, I am in awe of the wonders of your creation and how small I am in the scope of it all. Thank you for loving me, for listening to me, and for calling me your own.

LET GO

"Don't worry about tomorrow, because tomorrow will have its own worries. Each day has enough trouble of its own."

MATTHEW 6:34 NCV

Do you struggle with worry over what might happen tomorrow? Are you consumed with the unknowns you can't account for? It's normal to want to feel in control, but it's important to direct that desire toward something productive.

You can't control tomorrow's circumstances, but you can control your pursuit of God. He is the only one who has an accurate perspective of your life. Turn toward him when you worry, and he will give you peace. Lay your burdens at his feet and refuse to pick them up again. Trust him with your future because he is good, and he cares for you.

Faithful One, help me to let go of the need to know what tomorrow will bring. I don't want to live with that pressure. I choose to focus on today. I love you, and I trust you. I give you my worries, and I leave them there.

IN PROGRESS

It's time to be made new by every revelation that's been given to you.

Ephesians 4:23 TPT

In Christ, you have been made new, and you are continually being made new. Both things are true at the same time. You have been redeemed from the power of sin and death, and you are being continually transformed by the power of God's love.

You are not finished. Don't be discouraged by the parts of your life that don't look how you want. Every day is an opportunity for God to move in your heart and life. If you have surrendered to him, you are a work in progress, and he is not disappointed by how far you've come. Submit your life into his hands and trust his ability to get you where you need to go.

Wise God, I trust you to lead me. Thank you for continually transforming me in your presence. Remind me of your faithfulness when I am discouraged by my own progress.

WHAT YOU HAVE

"Silver or gold I do not have, but what I do have I give you. In the name of Jesus Christ of Nazareth, walk."

ACTS 3:6 NIV

You don't need riches or vast resources in order to make a meaningful impact in the lives of those around you. If you want to make a difference, whether with individuals or your community, use what you already have access to.

The greatest gift you can give someone is the love of Jesus. Introducing others to his power, kindness, grace, and mercy cannot be compared to piles of earthly treasures. You might feel empty-handed, but the way you walk alongside others with thoughtfulness and truth is far more meaningful than showering them with riches.

Lord, thank you for this day and for the opportunity to do good. Instead of looking at what I don't have, I open my eyes to what you have already given me.

EVERYTHING WE NEED

By his divine power, God has given us everything we need for living a godly life. We have received all of this by coming to know him, the one who called us to himself by means of his marvelous glory and excellence.

2 PETER 1:3 NLT

God gives you everything you need for living a life that pleases him and reflects his nature in the world. If you feel ill-equipped to love, he offers you his own. When you don't know how to keep going, he offers you his grace. Everything you need is found in fellowship with him.

Turn to the Lord whenever you come to the end of your own means. Ask him for what you lack. Take a moment to receive from his Spirit and then do what is yours to do. Trust him to cover your efforts. It's more important to be willing than perfect. Keep going and seek restoration when you make mistakes. All the treasures of God's love are in Christ, and you have more than enough to cover every area of your life.

Lord, thank you for providing everything I need to live a godly life. I humble myself before you. Be glorified in my life as I continually submit to you.

ALWAYS MORE

Grace, mercy and peace will be with us, from God the Father and from Jesus Christ, the Son of the Father, in truth and love.

2 John 1:3 NASB

God has not left you with a spirit of fear or of anxiety. He does not give you reason to fret or worry. He offers you generous grace, plenty of mercy, and unending peace. All you need to do is come to the Father through Jesus and ask him to pour out his presence over you through his Holy Spirit.

Turn to the Lord when the peace of your heart is challenged. Ask him for help when your strength is low and you notice your lack. Receive from the overflow of his loving heart. He always has more to offer in his rich presence. He never runs dry; he is an abundant source of all that you need.

Abundant God, there is no lack in you, and I will not stop coming to you with my need. I rely on your mercy, grace, and peace more than I can say. Thank you for the abundance in your love and in your presence.

FREEDOM ALL AROUND

The Lord is the Spirit, and where the Spirit of the Lord is, there is freedom.

2 Corinthians 3:17 CSB

There is freedom wherever the Spirit of the Lord is. He offers you liberation in every circumstance. When you feel backed into a corner, ask the Lord to show you what choices you actually have. He breaks down every barrier that could possibly keep you from his love, and he offers all you need to walk in the freedom of his Spirit.

The powerful liberty of Christ sets you free on the inside. He gives you space to heal. Christ's redemption sets your soul in wide-open places where you can rest, grow, and transform. Freedom is yours even now.

Spirit of God, thank you for bringing refreshing peace, powerful joy, and overwhelming freedom to my heart, soul, and spirit. You are my liberty, and I come alive in you.

POSSIBILITIES OF GRATITUDE

Give thanks in all circumstances; for this is the will of God in Christ Jesus for you.

1 Thessalonians 5:18 esv

Gratitude primes your heart and mind to look for the goodness of God in the world around you. Thankfulness helps you accept reality while holding hope for the possibilities of the future. There are a multitude of benefits to practicing gratitude. The more you notice goodness in your life, the more you will cultivate peace, joy, and hope.

Make gratitude a practice in your daily life and expect your heart to be transformed. Gratitude can exist simultaneously with grief, frustration, confusion, or despair. It is meant to exist despite your other feelings. You don't need to brush aside your emotions in favor of thanksgiving. You can process your raw feelings *and* practice gratitude.

Wonderful One, thank you for the air in my lungs and the sun in the sky. Thank you for life, for kindness, and for glimpses of your goodness. I will give thanks in every circumstance I encounter, remembering that you are with me through it all.

LIFEGIVING WISDOM

The excellence of knowledge is that wisdom gives life to those who have it.

ECCLESIASTES 7:12 NKJV

Wisdom is a resource that benefits those who possess it. Another translation says that wisdom protects just like money, but wisdom keeps its possessor alive. Money can protect you by providing for your practical needs, but wisdom is an even greater guard because it cannot be taken away from you.

Invest in the treasure of wisdom. Seek after it with all you have. Humbly embrace God's wisdom and deliberately apply it to your life. Look to Scripture for guidance and trust God for grace to hide truth in your heart. Run wholeheartedly after Jesus who is the personification of godly wisdom.

Wise One, I don't want to invest in things that fade away. I want to invest in your wisdom more than I do anything else. I choose to follow you, and I choose to cherish you and your leadership in my life.

ONLY GOD

"If people want to brag, let them brag
that they understand and know me.
Let them brag that I am the LORD,
and that I am kind and fair,
and that I do things that are right on earth.
This kind of bragging pleases me," says the LORD.

JEREMIAH 9:24 NCV

If you want to brag about anything, brag about the goodness of the Lord. He is kind and fair, and he does what is right. Though you might falter, he never does. Though you see in part, he knows everyone and everything through and through. Resist the urge to idolize your own opinions, for God is above them all.

Only God is perfect. Only he is righteous. Instead of lifting other people up on pedestals or praising your own accomplishments, humbly stand in awe of the Lord. He sees each of your successes, and his recognition is more than enough. His approval matters far more than anyone else's. Put God on the throne of your heart, and he will keep you grounded in humility and love.

God, you alone are worthy of my praise.

TRUE CHRIST

"Simply join your life with mine. Learn my ways and you'll discover that I'm gentle, humble, easy to please. You will find refreshment and rest in me."

MATTHEW 11:29 TPT

If the Jesus you know is demanding, easily upset, or completely unrelatable, then you have yet to discover the true Christ. He says that when you join your life with his, you will find that he is gentle, humble, and easy to please. You will find rest for your soul and refreshment for your heart in his presence.

Following Jesus is meant to bring relief from the pressures of this world. As you give him your burdens, he gives you freedom. As you lay your cares at his feet, he showers you with grace and mercy. Walking in his ways should not be tiresome, and you don't need to grit your teeth to please him. He offers you the joy of abundant life.

Prince of Peace, whenever I catch a glimpse of your kindness, I am struck by how wonderful you are. You are always better than I expect. Meet me today with the peace of your presence and the joy of your love.

POWERFUL BLESSINGS

"The Lord bless you and keep you;
the Lord make his face shine on you and be gracious to you;
the Lord turn his face toward you and give you peace."

Numbers 6:24-26 NIV

As you read today's verse, receive it first as a blessing over you. Perhaps put a hand over your heart as you read it over yourself. Allow yourself to receive the blessing fully in your heart. Invite the presence of God to expand your awareness of his nearness.

As you carry this blessing in your heart throughout your day, offer it as a gift for others as well. When you encounter people who put your patience to the test, remember this blessing and extend it to them, whether or not you speak a word of it. Bless each person you interact with today and thank God that you are able to give because you have so richly received from him.

Gracious God, thank you for the blessings I receive from knowing you. I won't withhold them from others today. Give me grace to freely share your love with others.

SOLID GROUND

This same God who takes care of me will supply all your needs from his glorious riches, which have been given to us in Christ Jesus.

PHILIPPIANS 4:19 NLT

God is a reliable help in every circumstance. He promises to supply your needs out of the abundance of his resources. You can trust him to do it. Instead of getting caught up in the worry of how you will make it through, you can trust God to cover what you are not able to. It is to your benefit to take him at his Word.

In Christ, you have all you need. You will find grace, strength, mercy, and peace in his fellowship. There is joy, hope, and faith in his presence. Run to him today and trust his faithful provision. Give him your anxieties and offer him your hand. He will pull you from the mud of worry and set your feet on solid ground.

Trustworthy One, I don't want to live under the constant stress of worry and what-ifs. Help me to be grounded in your faithfulness, provision, and wisdom. I know that you will take care of me.

DAILY DETERMINATION

He rescued us from the domain of darkness, and transferred us to the kingdom of His beloved Son, in whom we have redemption, the forgiveness of sins.

COLOSSIANS 1:13-14 NASB

Not only has Christ rescued you from the domain of darkness, but he has made you come alive through his resurrection power. He has given you victory over death, and he has equipped you to live a life that honors him. He has done a great miracle in your life, and he sustains it every day.

You are no longer a slave to sin. You are free to follow the Lord. The idea that you cannot change or that you are doomed to stay in destructive cycles is a lie. God has welcomed you into his kingdom, and he has empowered to live freely. Lay your burdens down daily and determine within your heart to cling to the truth.

Christ, thank you for removing the power that sin, fear, and death had over me. Thank you for welcoming me into your kingdom with mercy and grace. Give me strength to turn toward you each day.

ORDINARY PLACES

When Jesus came to the place, he looked up and said to him, "Zacchaeus, hurry and come down because today it is necessary for me to stay at your house."

Luke 19:5 CSB

When Zacchaeus climbed up into the tree to see over the crowds, he simply wanted to catch a glimpse of Jesus. He did not expect anything more than that, yet Jesus answered the hunger in his heart. Jesus saw his longing and responded with grace and mercy. Zacchaeus just wanted one look, yet Jesus honored him with the blessing of his presence.

Every little movement of your heart toward the Lord is seen by him. He honors it with more than you ask for or expect. He is exceedingly better than you could hope for. Allow the Lord to speak to your heart today and answer Him when you hear his voice. He loves to meet with you in the ordinary places you dwell.

Jesus, thank you for being and doing more than I expect. You are so gracious with me, and your presence is a relief and joy in every moment. Come to my home, enter my heart, and teach me your ways. I love you.

JULY

We know that all things work together for the good of those who love God, who are called according to his purpose.

Romans 8:28 CSB

SLEEP SOUNDLY

If you lie down, you will not be afraid;
when you lie down, your sleep will be sweet.

PROVERBS 3:24 ESV

You cannot expect the world around you to be a place of complete peace. However, you can expect God to stay with you no matter what your circumstances look like. You can know the powerful peace of God in your heart even as tensions rise around you.

God knows what your spirit and body need. He knows you need to rest and be refreshed on a daily basis. He promises to give you the gift of sweet sleep when you depend on him. As you close your eyes tonight, be mindful of the God's attentiveness toward you. He sees you, and he will watch over you.

Defender, I know that you are with me through every twist and turn of life. I don't have to prepare myself for the unknown, for you will do it. Help me rest sweetly and wake up refreshed.

OUT OF CAPTIVITY

He brought them out of darkness and the shadow of death,
And broke their chains in pieces.

PSALM 107:14 NKJV

Even before Jesus was resurrected and broke the chains of sin and death, God led his people out of captivity. Psalm 107 recounts the ways in which God delivered his people over and over again. The wonderful news for you today is that he still delivers his people out of darkness, shame, and bondage.

The Israelites were constantly waiting for God to come through for them. You have the incredible blessing of being able to lean on Jesus. His death and resurrection were the final and eternal sacrifice. You don't need anything else to be redeemed by God. You can lean on Christ's work fully for all of your days.

Redeemer, thank you for bringing me out of cycles of sin, shame, and fear. I'm so grateful you are the one who breaks chains and sets the captive free. I am free in your love because of all that you have done.

GOD KNOWS

"Whoever can be trusted with a little can also be trusted with a lot, and whoever is dishonest with a little is dishonest with a lot."

Luke 16:10 NCV

The principles of God's kingdom are clear and orderly. Scripture offers you advice and council for everything situation you might face. Today's verse is a reminder that God knows exactly what you can handle. He sees what you are capable of, and he orders your life accordingly.

You don't have to prove to God that you are strong. If he hasn't given you certain responsibilities, you can trust that he has a reason. In the same way, you can trust his guidance when you face situations that seem out of your capabilities. He knows exactly what you can handle and what you cannot. Your ability to lean on him for strength is more important than whether or not you think you can handle something.

Wise God, thank you your constant presence in my life. Thank you for giving me the wisdom necessary to walk through each of my days. I trust you to lead me, and I trust you to watch over me.

OPEN HEARTS

"Those who listen with open hearts will receive more revelation. But those who don't listen with open hearts will lose what little they think they have!"

MARK 4:25 TPT

An open heart that loves to learn will receive more revelation. A closed-off heart cannot grow in understanding. If you refuse to consider other perspectives, you're missing out on the possibility of something beautiful. It is important to your development that you remain receptive and open to learning new things. This is true in life and in spirituality.

Children know that they have more to learn. Perhaps this is why Jesus encouraged his followers to be like little children. They are constantly learning, growing, and adapting. You can do the same thing as you remain humble before God and others.

Jesus, I want to grow in understanding, and I know that requires a humble and open heart. Help me to let go of fear that keeps my heart closed off to hearing what is necessary for growth. I humble myself before you and others today.

TELL YOUR STORY

Let the redeemed of the LORD tell their story.

PSALM 107:2 NIV

If you are in Christ, you have a story to tell. How has his love transformed your life? How has his wisdom changed the way that you live? Spend some time with the Lord today, asking for the Spirit to show you the power of his powerful mercy in specific areas of your life.

As you recall what God has done for you, think about how you can share your experience with others. You have a unique testimony of God's goodness. His faithfulness in your life can encourage those around you. Speak boldly and give God the credit for every blessing you have.

Christ Jesus, thank you for the power of your redemption in my life. Spirit, reveal the thread of your mercy in my life and remind me of your power in specific areas of my life. I want to share the incredible power of your love with others today.

GRACIOUS FREEDOM

Sin is no longer your master, for you no longer live under the requirements of the law. Instead, you live under the freedom of God's grace.

ROMANS 6:14 NLT

What does it truly mean to live under the freedom of God's grace? Think about the possibilities. There are no limits to God's grace, so you don't have to fear disappointing him. Even when you mess up in major ways, God receives you with love as you humbly come to him. He will not hold your sin against you.

You are free to live under the light of God's love without anything hindering you. Take any area of your life that feels bound by obligation or shame and submit it to the Lord. Allow him to examine your heart and show you where you aren't living freely.

Gracious Father, thank you for lifting the weight of sin, fear, and shame that held me back from living fully under your love. I am free in your grace, and I am undone by the power of your love.

LISTEN WELL

You know this, my beloved brothers and sisters.
Now everyone must be quick to hear, slow to speak,
and slow to anger.

JAMES 1:19 NASB

One of the best ways to honor the people in your life is to listen well. Everyone feels noticed and cared for when their words are carefully absorbed rather than brushed over. People feel loved when you listen to understand rather than listening to respond.

If you feel the constant urge to make your opinion known, perhaps it's time to evaluate your heart. Is there part of you that feels overlooked or ignored? Do you worry that your voice won't be heard? Take any discrepancies to the Lord and allow him to shower his extravagant love upon you. As you find your belonging in his presence, you'll find more confidence to be a thoughtful and intentional listener.

Wise God, I'm so grateful that your ways are better than mine. You see my heart, and you know exactly where I can grow in love. Teach me how to listen well. I want my actions to make other people feel loved and cared for.

CONFIDENCE TO CONTINUE

"When you pass through the waters,
I will be with you,
and the rivers will not overwhelm you.
When you walk through the fire,
you will not be scorched,
and the flame will not burn you."

ISAIAH 43:2 CSB

God's gracious presence is your peace and your guide. He will not leave you or forsake you. He is steady when the flood waters rise or fire burns hot. He promises to be with you through it all. You don't need to be afraid of fierce weather or the storms of life.

God is your confidence to keep going. You don't need to shrink back when the winds of testing blow. God's faithful presence gives you courage to persevere through hard times. His presence is your comfort and your strength. When you feel threatened by your circumstances, remember that the existence of trials does not mean God has left you.

Spirit, thank you for being with me every moment of every day. I rely on your leadership, your perspective, and your strength.

LET GOD

It depends not on human will or exertion, but on God, who has mercy.

ROMANS 9:16 ESV

If God chooses when to show mercy, then you can neither earn it nor lose it. This should be a welcome relief especially when you are tired of striving for your place. Your place is secure in Christ's kingdom, and you don't have to strive for anything.

When you learn to let go of your need to prove yourself, you can rest in the mercy of God. He knows you through and through, and he chose to show you mercy when you were at your worst. Give up the urge to make yourselves worthy and live freely in response to God's gracious gift. Instead of reaching for an unattainable mark today, live in the peace that is yours through Christ.

Merciful God, I want to give up striving to prove myself to you and others. In you, I am already enough because you love me. You have offered the fullness of your grace, mercy, and salvation already. What else is there to gain?

OBEDIENCE IS BETTER

"Has the LORD as great delight in burnt offerings and sacrifices, as in obeying the voice of the LORD? Behold, to obey is better than sacrifice, and to heed than the fat of rams."

1 SAMUEL 15:22 NKJV

It is more pleasing to the Lord to obey what he says rather than offering sacrifices. He cares more about the state of your heart than your idea of acceptable behavior. He longs for you to offer him your life out of faithful obedience.

God wants you to trust him as a friend rather than a strict master you're afraid of disappointing. He wants you to experience his kindness and gentleness. He wants the intimacy of a relationship with you over the coldness of obligated compliance. If all he wanted were sacrifices, he could create those himself. He wants your soft and authentic heart.

Gracious God, I am so grateful for fellowship with you. Remind me of the value of relationship when I fall into patterns of obligation. Keep my heart soft and turned toward you.

HE IS NOT BEHIND

The Lord is not slow in doing what he promised—the way some people understand slowness. But God is being patient with you. He does not want anyone to be lost, but he wants all people to change their hearts and lives.

2 Peter 3:9 NCV

God is more patient with you than you can comprehend. He knows exactly what your life will look like. If you surrender to him, you can trust that he is capable of managing your growth. He knows how you learn, and he is able to transform your heart whenever needed.

You are not a failure, and you are not behind. God is the one who graciously transforms you with his love. In his presence you are molded and shaped into his likeness. He sees you perfectly, and he knows what you need. Remember that his kindness, not your own ability, drew you to him in the first place. Let go of your own perceptions and trust God to fulfill each of his promises.

Lord, thank you for your present grace and mercy that is working out your purposes on the earth and in my life. I trust you to lead me because I know you will keep your promises.

IN LIGHT OF ETERNITY

We view our slight, short-lived troubles in the light of eternity. We see our difficulties as the substance that produces for us an eternal, weighty glory far beyond all comparison.

2 Corinthians 4:17 TPT

Broadening your perspective beyond your current reality can help you stay grounded. You're your eyes heavenward and remember that there is more going on than you are capable of understanding. Today's struggles won't seem like such a big deal when you have the big picture in mind.

When frustrations arise, remember that they will not last. Learn to view your troubles as opportunities to persevere in grace, knowing that they produce eternal glory. When this short life is over, you will enter into the fullness of eternity. What a glorious hope this is.

Lord, help me keep my problems in perspective today, remembering that you are above them all. You are not fazed by the things that faze me. I'm so grateful for this.

CAPABLE HANDS

The eternal God is your refuge,
and underneath are the everlasting arms.

DEUTERONOMY 33:27 NIV

When the pressures of life feel as if they are too much to bear, lean back into the everlasting arms of your heavenly Father. He is right there. He will hold you up with his love, and he will be your refuge and source of peace.

You don't have to struggle alone in any area of your life today. Whenever you feel overwhelmed, close your eyes for a moment and picture yourself leaning back into God. Imagine his arms under yours, holding you up. He is more than strong enough to carry you. Your burdens could never be too much for him. Allow your soul to rest in his presence even as you continue about your day. You are not alone.

Eternal God, I rely on your help today. I lean back into your capable arms and trust you to do what I cannot. Thank you.

COURAGE TO COME

Let us come boldly to the throne of our gracious God. There we will receive his mercy, and we will find grace to help us when we need it most.

HEBREWS 4:16 NLT

There is no reason to withhold your heart from God today. You are fully embraced by him whenever you come to him. He promises to receive you with arms wide open. Whenever you need mercy, he offers you a fresh portion from his presence. When you need his help, there is an abundance of grace available to you.

Recognize whatever ideas hinder you from wholeheartedly and confidently coming before the Lord. Acknowledge lies you might be believing about his character. Remember that your thoughts dictate your actions. If you are thinking about God incorrectly, you will also interact with him incorrectly. Allow him to pull shame, fear, or doubt from your heart and run to him freely and confidently.

Merciful Lord, I don't want to keep myself from coming to you. I know you see me fully and love me extravagantly. Give me courage to run to you with boldness.

THROUGH CHRIST

The Law was given through Moses; grace and truth were realized through Jesus Christ.

JOHN 1:17 NASB

Jesus himself said that he came to fulfill the Law that was given to Moses. He met every requirement of the Law and shifted what is required of you. Instead of being bound to a list of standards, you have the freedom of being covered by his love. Now, your highest requirement is to love God and love others.

If you find comfort in following rules, you might struggle with the freedom Christ offers you. Remember that you are accountable to Jesus not a check list of standards. You honor him by operating with love, grace, and mercy in all you do. When you feel the urge to quantify your salvation by following rules, remember that Christ's sacrifice alone fulfilled the law and saved you.

Christ Jesus, in you is the fullness of grace and truth. I come to you with hunger in my heart to know you more. Minister to me as I spend time in your Word and in your presence.

POWERFUL LOVE

"I give you a new command: love one another. Just as I have loved you, you are also to love one another."

JOHN 13:34 CSB

God never requires anything from you that he hasn't already offered you. This is almost too great a truth to comprehend. He has already given you everything you need. The love you are to live by is already yours through Christ. You can love others because he first loved you.

When you feel as if you are running low on grace and love, turn your heart toward God and receive from his fullness. Ask him to fill you with all you need. Then, out of the overflow of his provision, you can offer to others what God has offered you. Your relationship with him is a never-ending cycle of reliance because he never runs dry.

Gracious God, thank you for the power of your love that fuels my own. Expand my understanding of your goodness and transform me in your presence. I am in awe of you.

OPEN MINDS

Then he opened their minds to understand the Scriptures.

LUKE 24:45 ESV

God's Spirit opens your mind to understand the Scriptures. He moves in you to reveal his power and truth. He gives you clarity and understanding to see him rightly. He helps you understand his character and his purposes. Through the Holy Spirit, he gives you the ability to comprehend the mystery of the gospel.

Scripture is not over your head. It's not too complicated, boring, or irrelevant. Every part of it is useful and powerful. If you've brushed over certain parts in the past, ask God for fresh revelation. Ask him to help you understand the Word and he will faithfully guide you. He will give you eyes to see, a mind to absorb truth, and a heart to understand.

Wise God, give me revelation of the truth of who you are in new and deeper ways today. Reveal what only you can and give me a greater understanding of the Word. Thank you.

OTHERS FIRST

A generous person will prosper;
whoever refreshes others will be refreshed.

Proverbs 11:25 NIV

The world will constantly tell you to take care of yourself. They will tell you to prioritize self-care and to always put yourself first. While some measure of this is okay, the message as a whole doesn't line up with Scripture. Scripture doesn't say to abandon all of your practical needs, but it does say that true refreshment is found by refreshing others.

It might seem counterintuitive, but lifting up others has the potential to renew your own energy. God promises to take care of those who lay down their lives for others. He sees the sacrifices you make, and he will not leave you empty handed. Boldly encourage others in a world that urges you to only look out for yourself.

Savior, you know more than anyone what it means to lay your life down. Give me grace to refresh others before myself. I trust you to take care of me as I seek to care for others.

THE RIGHT THING

"We don't want to upset these tax collectors. So go to the lake and fish. After you catch the first fish, open its mouth and you will find a coin. Take that coin and give it to the tax collectors for you and me."

MATTHEW 17:27 NCV

Jesus knew that if his disciples caught fish without paying taxes that the tax collectors would be upset. Jesus did not encourage rebellion or blatant disregard for the law. Instead, he encouraged his disciples to do the right thing and to trust God for what they lacked. You can do the same thing today.

When you find yourself wanting to cut corners, ask yourself if it is truly the right thing to do. Jesus always encouraged integrity. He set the example of living righteously rather than perfectly. He empowered his followers to be without fault and to represent God with strong character. You too can follow his leadership and trust him with the rest.

Jesus, thank you for the power of your wisdom that instructs me how to live. I want to live in integrity, honoring you and your name in all that I do. Thank you for the strength to do the right thing.

DEEPENING FRIENDSHIP

Look at how much encouragement you've found in your relationship with the Anointed One! You are filled to overflowing with his comforting love. You have experienced a deepening friendship with the Holy Spirit and have felt his tender affection and mercy.

PHILIPPIANS 2:1 TPT

Read through today's verse again. Have you experienced what Paul describes in fellowship with the Anointed One? Have you known encouragement, relief, and comfort in his love? How have you experienced a deepening friendship with the Holy Spirit?

You were created to fellowship with the Creator. You were made to know him and be fully known by him. Love is the basis of all that he did, does, and will do. Know that there is an invitation to you today to deepen your friendship with God through his Holy Spirit. Mercy and tender affection can be found in his presence. You will never reach the end of it.

Holy Spirit, I want to grow closer to you today. I am so encouraged by the clear invitation I have to know the Father and the Son. I am overwhelmed by the reality of your presence in my life.

NO NEED TO FEAR

The LORD is my light and my salvation—
whom shall I fear?
The LORD is the stronghold of my life—
of whom shall I be afraid?

PSALM 27:1 NIV

The Lord is your faithful light. When he asks you to follow him, he doesn't leave you alone in the dark. He is the source of your salvation, and he defends you with each step you take. Even when threats arise, you do not have to give into fear. As you continue to follow the leading of the Lord, he surrounds and protects you.

Knowing that God is with you, why would you choose to run from him? He is your source of perfect peace, life-giving love, and overwhelming hope. He is your strong and mighty defender, and he does not grow tired or weak. No matter what you face, God is by your side.

Faithful One, I trust that your light never dims, and your knowledge is never faulty. You are strong to save, and you always will be. I stick close to you, for you are my help in every season of the soul.

PATIENT CONFIDENCE

If we look forward to something we don't yet have, we must wait patiently and confidently.

ROMANS 8:25 NLT

When Paul talks about waiting patiently and confidently, he is talking about the fulfillment of God's promises. He's talking about our final redemption and the second coming of Christ. He urges believers to let anticipation for that day be their motivation for staying faithful to Jesus.

Waiting patiently and confidently doesn't mean you won't ever waver. It means that when you do, you turn your attention back to the Lord. It's okay if you have to remind yourself daily of what matters and what your goals are. Standing firmly on God's promises doesn't mean you won't have troubles. It means you have a firm foundation to stand upon when troubles do come. Turn your eyes to the Lord and look forward to the fulfillment of his promises.

Righteous One, I believe that you will follow through on every promise you have made. Fill me with confident hope. Give me patience as I wait for you to move.

MIGHTY PROTECTOR

The Lord watches over strangers;
He supports the fatherless and the widow,
But He thwarts the way of the wicked.

Psalm 146:9 NASB

God watches over strangers and immigrants. He supports widows and the fatherless. God protects people without the means to protect themselves. He is mindful of the helpless and those who are overlooked by society. With this in mind, you can ask yourself if you are diligently caring for those God cares for.

God is better than any ruler or influential leader history has ever known. His motives are pure, and his standards are perfect. When you begin to excuse your own lack of practical love toward your neighbor, remember what God calls you to. May you find yourself standing with God in humble obedience, caring for those whom he cares about.

Lord, empower me to love those who are overlooked. Help me to treat other people with the same mercy and grace you shower on me. Soften my heart and expand my ability to love like you do.

PERFECT GUIDANCE

Your ears shall hear a word behind you, saying,
"This is the way, walk in it,"
Whenever you turn to the right hand
Or whenever you turn to the left."

ISAIAH 30:21 NKJV

God offers you guidance every day. He is willing to tell you which steps to take. You don't need to flounder through your life on unsure footing. You can listen for his voice and confidently trust that he will speak. He loves to comfort, teach, encourage, and lead you. It is one of his greatest joys to walk with you through life.

You are not a burden to God. He is not annoyed that you don't know which way to go. He doesn't expect you to have directions memorized or to know the route through every problem. He would rather you depend on him for guidance than independently go about your business. Take advantage of his offer to lead you today. Take a deep breath and allow him to have control.

Good God, I trust your guidance. Teach me how to lean on you for each step I take. Thank you for keeping me safe and making my path clear.

SHARE THE GOODNESS

"Go back to your home, and tell all that God has done for you." And off he went, proclaiming throughout the town how much Jesus had done for him.

Luke 8:39 CSB

When God moves in your life, don't be afraid to share it with others. Boldly declare what God has done, knowing that it will encourage and bless those around you. Don't be ashamed of your experiences when God can use them to cultivate freedom and strengthen faith.

Your story might be exactly what someone else needs to hear. When God does a work of healing in your heart, it's worth sharing. When he restores what was broken or redeems what was lost, don't be embarrassed to celebrate and give him the credit he is due. As you glorify him in your weakness, you can encourage others to do the same.

Lord, I don't want to keep your good work to myself. Give me courage to share what you've done in my life. I worship you for all you've done and are yet to do.

YOUR CHOICE

"No one takes it from me, but I lay it down of my own accord. I have authority to lay it down, and I have authority to take it up again. This charge I have received from my Father."

JOHN 10:18 ESV

You are never truly powerless in any circumstance. You can choose how you will walk through the trials you face. You can choose to have a victim mindset, or you can be empowered by God's strength. When you ruminate on your problems and feel sorry for yourself, you miss out on the opportunity to experience the confidence of surrender.

Even Jesus was not a victim. He knew the plan of the Father was for him to lay his life down. He knew the suffering he would encounter, and he still didn't wallow in disappointment. He looked toward God with trust and confidence, knowing that the suffering would be worth the glory to come. In the same way, you have a choice in how you react to trials. You are not powerless or helpless. Partner with God and allow him to lead you through whatever comes your way.

Lord Jesus, thank you for the reminder that I am not powerless in my life. Though I cannot control what tomorrow will bring, I can choose how I show up in the world.

STRENGTH TRAINING

You are rich in everything—in faith, in speaking, in knowledge, in truly wanting to help, and in the love you learned from us. In the same way, be strong also in the grace of giving.

2 Corinthians 8:7 NCV

You are probably familiar with the ways you can train your muscles to become stronger through exercise. It takes consistency, practice, and hard work to strengthen your physical muscles. The same is true of your emotional and spiritual muscles.

Did you know that you can strengthen your spiritual muscles in practical ways? Paul lays out some of the strengths of the Corinthian church in today's verse. He also points out an area where they can grow stronger. He encourages them to grow in the grace of giving. As you practice practical generosity, doing the hard work of following through and being consistent, your giving will grow strong in the grace of God.

Lord, I forget sometimes how practical you are. I don't want to waste away the opportunities I have thinking that my actions don't matter. Help me to be self-disciplined, wise, and gracious in generosity.

CHOOSE WELL

Beloved ones, God has called us to live a life of freedom. But don't view this wonderful freedom as an excuse to set up a base of operations in the natural realm. Constantly love each other and be committed to serve one another.

GALATIANS 5:13 TPT

The freedom you have in Christ is not an excuse to do whatever you want. Instead, God asks you to use your freedom for the benefit of others. He calls you to love well and serve wholeheartedly. Be wary of following a partial gospel where you follow your own desires and claim God's grace.

Jesus knows that you are prone to do what you want. He knows you are likely to wander away. He knows each of your weaknesses and he sets you free anyway. He sees your acts of defiance and still willingly lays his life down for you. This is why he gently urges you to focus on loving well and serving those around you. Respond to his gracious gift by laying your life down as he did.

Lord, thank you for the freedom I have in you. Give me grace to use that freedom for the benefit of others. Keep me from pridefully going my own way. Teach me how to selflessly lay my life down.

IMPOSSIBLE LOVE

Live in harmony with one another. Do not be proud, but be willing to associate with people of low position. Do not be conceited.

Romans 12:16 NIV

On some days it seems impossible to love. Thankfully, God isn't hindered by our frame of possibility. Some people are difficult to deal with and some situations are uncomfortable. It's not always fun to lay your life down for the sake of someone else. It's painful to set your preferences aside, and it takes maturity to peacefully engage with people who push your buttons.

Though you might not enjoy the company of everyone you meet, you are still called to love them. The good news is that God is the one who empowers you to do this. He doesn't ask you to love out of your own ability. He simply asks you to share his love with those around you. If you ask him to help you, he will joyfully equip you to walk in his ways.

Worthy One, when my pride keeps me from loving others well, change my perspective with your wisdom. I know that I am no better than anyone else. Help me to love others despite how I might feel at the moment.

READY TO FORGIVE

O Lord, you are so good, so ready to forgive,
so full of unfailing love for all who ask for your help.

Psalm 86:5 NLT

God is full of unfailing love and mercy. He is ready to restore you when you come to him. He is so very good. You can call on God constantly without fear that he will turn you away. He always welcomes you with open arms. He will help you whenever you ask him for support.

When you receive the mercy of God, you are able to offer that same mercy to others. Scripture says that those who are forgiven much will forgive others. In other words, you can freely share whatever God has given you. As you experience the depths of his mercy, you be merciful toward others.

Merciful One, your love knows no bounds. Thank you for helping me every time I cry out to you. As you intervene on my behalf, may I expand in my ability to love others. Help me share your grace and mercy with everyone I come across.

DON'T BE ENSNARED

The fear of man brings a snare,
But one who trusts in the LORD will be protected.

PROVERBS 29:25 NASB

When you fully trust in the Lord, you can let go of the fear of man. You can freely ignore the opinions of others in favor of God's opinion. You can look to him for wisdom instead of frantically searching the internet or your social circles for validation. You can graciously excuse yourself from harsh debates knowing that God alone can bring about justice and compassion on the earth.

Don't allow the passionate opinions of others to sway you from God's sovereignty. No matter how loud the world yells, God's truth will remain. No matter how much people fight or disagree, God remains unshaken and enthroned. You can look to him with quiet trust instead of worrying about the dissension and lack of peace in the world around you.

Lord, thank you for your steadfast love that fuels my trust. You are better than anyone else, so why would I be intimidated by others? Help me, Lord, to be free from the fear of man. I trust in you.

AUGUST

"When you pray, go into your private room, shut your door, and pray to your Father who is in secret."

MATTHEW 6:6 CSB

IMAGE OF THE ALMIGHTY

The Son is the radiance of God's glory and the exact expression of his nature, sustaining all things by his powerful word. After making purification for sins, he sat down at the right hand of the Majesty on high.

HEBREWS 1:3 CSB

Jesus is the living expression of God's true nature. He is the fullness of God in human form. If you want to know God, look at who Christ revealed him to be. As a follower of Jesus, you have the honor of knowing God through Christ's example, Scripture, and the fellowship of the Holy Spirit.

There is always more to discover about God, and there is nothing standing in your way. You have unlimited access to his presence. Look at your time with him as an opportunity to broaden your perspective and learn more about him. Be awed by his nature, bowing down before him with each fresh revelation.

Jesus Christ, I want to know you more today. Reveal the majesty of your love and truth to my heart and mind today. I look to you.

LIFT YOUR FOCUS

If then you have been raised with Christ, seek the things that are above, where Christ is, seated at the right hand of God. Set your minds on things that are above, not on things that are on earth.

Colossians 3:1-2 ESV

Christ's resurrection is also your resurrection. He is seated above the realm of this world, enthroned in power, honor, and authority. This is why it's important to look above the trappings of this world to seek his higher perspective.

Instead of getting weighed down by the distractions of this world, set your heart and mind on the things that matter most. Pay attention to the object of your gaze and ask yourself if it has eternal value. True satisfaction comes from devoting your life to the values and purposes of Christ's kingdom rather than your own.

Lord Jesus, I don't want to be bogged down by the temporary things of this world that don't truly matter. Help me to keep my focus on you and your ways.

SEASONS FOR EVERYTHING

To everything there is a season,
A time for every purpose under heaven.

ECCLESIASTES 3:1 NKJV

Nothing is wasted in the kingdom of God. You are not ahead or behind, no matter how you may feel at this stage in your life. There are seasons for sowing and seasons for reaping. Even when you are in a season that feels dormant, there is always growth ahead.

Whatever you are experiencing right now will not last forever. Circumstances change and so will you. You'll gain perspective, grow in wisdom, and change your mind. No part of your life is stagnant. When you surrender yourself to the Lord, you can trust that as seasons shift and change you will be steadily transformed into his likeness.

Lord, help me see the beauty that is hidden within each season. Help me to embrace the lessons of the season I am in right now.

ENJOY YOURSELF

People ought to enjoy every day of their lives,
no matter how long they live.

Ecclesiastes 11:8 NCV

If you don't take time to enjoy the ordinary parts of life, you will miss out on the joy of contentment. You can choose to look at the repetitive details of your days as boring, or you can see them as a gift. You are the only one who can enjoy your life.

Comparison and sensationalism will steal your joy. If you base the value of your life on exciting, monumental, or brag worthy moments, you'll spend your days aiming for a moving target. There is beauty in the hundreds of small blessings God has showered on you. Quiet contentment comes from seeing every moment, big or small, as extraordinary.

Lord, delight comes from you. Show me how joyful you are. Help me see the beauty in my ordinary life.

NOTHING IS IMPOSSIBLE

How great is our God!
There's absolutely nothing his power cannot accomplish,
and he has infinite understanding of everything.

Psalm 147:5 TPT

The God who put the planets in motion is the one overlooks each of your days. Nothing is too overwhelming for him. His power can accomplish whatever he likes. He can do so much more than you could ever imagine.

Do you have any impossible situations? Are there parts of your life you've given up on and written off as a burden you'll always bear? Take time today to recommit your biggest frustrations to God. His timing is perfect, and he is absolutely able to accomplish what you need. Trust him once again with that issue you've gotten tired of praying about.

Majestic One, I believe that there is nothing outside of your grasp. I join with the vastness of your love and ask for breakthrough. Thank you.

UNQUENCHABLE LOVE

Many waters cannot quench love;
rivers cannot sweep it away.
If one were to give all the wealth of one's house for love,
it would be utterly scorned.

SONG OF SOLOMON 8:7 NIV

God's love is fierce and strong. It is an unstoppable force that both stands firmly and advances in unending measures. All the treasures of this world would be like a speck of dust in comparison to the value of his pure love.

No matter what you are facing today, the rushing river of God's love floods over and through it. You are never without the love of God, and you cannot escape it. Whatever you walk through today, you do it with the power of God's affection and mercy. He is your source, strength, and oasis.

Merciful Father, I have only tasted of your love, but it has changed my life. I want to be continually transformed as you flood my awareness with your affection. I am yours, Lord, and I pour my love back on you.

TAKE A BREAK

The apostles returned to Jesus from their ministry tour and told him all they had done and taught. Then Jesus said, "Let's go off by ourselves to a quiet place and rest awhile." He said this because there were so many people coming and going that Jesus and his apostles didn't even have time to eat.

MARK 6:30-31 NLT

When Jesus' followers returned to him after ministering to others, he invited them to find a secluded place to rest awhile. He knew the power of rest for their souls and bodies. If Jesus, the perfect example of God's character, can embrace rest then you can too.

When was the last time you truly took a break from the responsibilities of life? Do you remember the last time you set your burdens at the cross and enjoyed the soul rest that comes from surrender? It's important to rest physically and spiritually. Today, find ways to refresh your soul, heart, mind, and body.

Creator, I want to take your invitation to rest seriously. Help me to put aside the endless demands of work and family and create a day where I can truly be refreshed each week.

PEOPLE OF HIS PASTURE

Know that the LORD Himself is God;
It is He who has made us, and not we ourselves;
We are His people and the sheep of His pasture.

PSALM 100:3 NASB

If the Lord is your God, then you are among the people of his pasture. Don't hesitate to enter his presence with joy. Run into his courts with thanksgiving. Keep your heart soft to his correction, and trust that he knows how to take care of you just as a shepherd cares perfectly for his sheep.

Lean on the strength and expertise of your good Shepherd. Remember that he knows you inside and out. He knows your strengths and weaknesses even better than you do. He knows what you need to survive, and he knows what you need to flourish. Surrender your life into his care and relax knowing that you are safe in his fold.

Yahweh, I am yours. I am your child. Thank you for making me as I am, and for advising me in my growth. I love you more than I can say.

SPEAKER OF TRUTH

Putting away lying, speak the truth, each one to his neighbor, because we are members of one another.

EPHESIANS 4:25 CSB

You are responsible for the words you say. As a follower of Jesus, you are encouraged to be truthful in everything you say. Don't give in to the desire to encourage, embellish, or lie. Be honest and transparent.

Your honest and authentic words are a gift to the people around you. Honesty requires humility, and humility generates vulnerability. When you admit that you don't know everything, you leave space for other people to share their wisdom and experiences. This helps cultivate intimacy and trust.

Lord, I want to be known as a speaker of the truth and as a reliable and loving friend. I don't want to hide behind false pretenses or insecurity. Help me to stand on truth and be honest in all I say.

CHECK YOUR HEART

Let each one test his own work, and then his reason to boast will be in himself alone and not in his neighbor. For each will have to bear his own load.

GALATIANS 6:4-5 ESV

When you are too concerned with the actions of others, you risk overlooking your own responsibilities. You can't focus on what God has given you to do if you are constantly worried about the failures and successes of others. It's easy to point fingers, but it's more difficult to take personal responsibility for your own life.

Staying in your own lane will cultivate peace and contentment in your life. The more you refuse to get lost in comparison, the more joy you will find in God's unique path for you. He carefully orchestrates each person's life including your own. Turn toward your heavenly Father and humbly accept what he has asked you to do.

Lord, when I am quick to judge how others fail, remind me that I should first look at my own life. Thank you for your grounded wisdom.

HE GETS IT

We do not have a high priest who cannot sympathize with our weaknesses, but was in all points tempted as we are, yet without sin.

HEBREWS 4:15 NKJV

Jesus walked this earth as a man. He was born into poverty, grew up with siblings, and spent time in the wilderness being tempted. He knows full well what the limitations of humanity are. He knows the reality of exhaustion, grief, and disappointment.

How have you been able to relate to Jesus in his humanity? Have you discovered relief in knowing that he understands weakness? He didn't sin, but he doesn't throw that in your face. Instead, he is strong where you are weak. He offers you liberation and redemption. He is well aware of your downfalls, and he more than compensated for them at the cross.

Jesus, sometimes I forget that you were an actual man who had to deal with hunger, conflict, and temptation. Thank you for coming to earth to reveal the heart of the Father and for doing it as a human so that I can relate to you.

GOD'S DESIRE

The Lord wants to show his mercy to you.
He wants to rise and comfort you.
The Lord is a fair God,
and everyone who waits for his help will be happy.

Isaiah 30:18 NCV

God wants to rise and comfort you. Where the world focuses on never-ending self-care, God calls you to submit yourself to his care. His desire is for you to experience his mercy on a daily basis. He doesn't expect you to perfectly manage everything on your own.

When life feels like too much and you're not sure you can take another step, run toward God's presence. Instead of searching for refreshment on your own, look to God. Time with him will do more for your soul than any habit, practice, or treat you can manufacture. You need his presence more than anything else.

Lord, I want to receive your mercy, to be comforted by your presence, and to be regenerated by your kindness today. Thank you for taking such good care of me.

TRUE WISDOM

If you consider yourself to be wise and one who understands the ways of God, advertise it with a beautiful, fruitful life guided by wisdom's gentleness. Never brag or boast about what you've done and you'll prove that you're truly wise.

James 3:13 TPT

Wisdom that comes from God is quiet and humble. It does not insist on its own way, and it does not make other people feel as if they don't measure up. Wisdom that comes from God doesn't brag about its success or claim to have all the answers. Wisdom that comes from God speaks for itself.

When you honor God with your actions, your life will display his love. You don't have to convince anyone that you are doing the right thing. Let go of the desire to look a certain way and be content with honoring the Lord with each step you take. A quiet and gentle display of God's character shows more maturity than boasting in your own ability.

Wise God, forgive me for how I have been impressed by those with power, prestige, and big egos. I want to emulate the truth and power of your gentle and humble wisdom.

UNCONFINED

"I am the LORD, the God of all mankind.
Is anything too hard for me?"

JEREMIAH 32:27 NIV

God is not restricted by anything. He is not intimidated by the things that are too hard for you to do. Instead of doubting according to your own understanding, allow his majesty to expand your expectations. Your faith will grow as you look toward him with confidence, trusting that he can do far more than you ever imagined.

Have you allowed your limitations to impact how you see God? It is human nature to project your own experiences, strengths, and weaknesses onto others. When it comes to God, you can't judge him based on your perspective. His greatness goes far beyond anything you can compare it to.

Lord God, I believe that you are better than I can imagine. Open my eyes to see you in ways I haven't before.

ALONE TIME

After sending them home, he went up into the hills by himself to pray. Night fell while he was there alone.

MATTHEW 14:23 NLT

Jesus knew the importance of alone time. He knew his human limits, and he spent time alone to pray to his Father and find refreshment. Don't feel guilty for needing breaks away from people, even from those you love. Breaks are necessary and can give you renewed love, vision, and energy.

Try to incorporate breaks into your daily routine. Take time to deliberately seek the Lord. This doesn't have to take hours or be complicated in any way. Seeking him intentionally can be as simple as taking a few extra minutes in the morning to commit your day to him or taking the long way home from work so you can pray in the car. There are always extra pockets of time you can devote to God.

Jesus, thank you for your example of embracing solitude. Give me the discipline necessary to step away from the crowd and seek the Father.

CREATING CONTENTMENT

Not that I speak from need, for I have learned to be content in whatever circumstances I am.

PHILIPPIANS 4:11 NASB

If you've ever chased satisfaction, you know it's a fruitless pursuit. Even when you get what you want, it's likely that you will quickly move on to another desire. The goal post for man-made happiness is always moving. The true secret to being content is knowing that it has nothing to do with what you do or do not have.

Contentment comes from trusting Jesus in all circumstances. It comes from knowing that his love is the richest treasure you will ever have. Deep, soul-filling satisfaction comes from the pursuit of the one who made you. He alone can give you your heart's desires.

God, thank you for the power of your presence that never fades or diminishes. You are fully with me every moment. That is the greatest gift of all. Thank you.

NEVER TOO LATE

Boaz took Ruth, and she became his wife. And he went in to her, and the LORD gave her conception, and she bore a son. Then the women said to Naomi, "Blessed be the LORD, who has not left you this day without a redeemer, and may his name be renowned in Israel!"

RUTH 4:13-14 ESV

God is a God of restoration. Even when everything seems lost, your story is not over. Even when you can't see past your current struggles, the best is yet to come. There is no situation that is too desolate for God to redeem.

God sees you at all times, but he is especially aware of you when you are suffering. He is beside you as you grieve, and he comforts you when you are surrounded by darkness. When life takes an unexpected turn, he does not leave you alone to navigate uncharted water. Remember that he sees each of your days, and you don't need to worry because he is for you.

Redeemer, thank you that my best years are not behind me. Though I have had goodness in my life, I know there is even more coming as you produce new fruit out of the ashes of my disappointment. I trust you.

ABSOLUTELY INSEPARABLE

I am persuaded that neither death nor life, nor angels nor rulers, nor things present nor things to come, nor powers, nor height nor depth, nor any other created thing will be able to separate us from the love of God that is in Christ Jesus our Lord.

Romans 8:38-39 CSB

Absolutely nothing can separate you from the love of God. Christ has bridged every gap there ever was, and there is no stopping the power of his love. There is great comfort and confidence to be found in the steadiness of God's love for you.

Seasons will change but God's love remains. You will have both successes and failures, but God's love does not ebb and flow. The circumstances of life might take you by surprise, but God's love is always predictable. When you cannot depend on anything or anyone, God's love is always reliable.

Christ Jesus, thank you for the power of your love that overcame everything put in its path. There isn't anything keeping me from the fullness of your mercy today. Flood me in your presence and love me to life again.

YOUR PORTION

My flesh and my heart fail;
But God is the strength of my heart and my portion forever.

Psalm 73:26 NKJV

Even when your own heart and flesh fails, God does not. No matter how you change or age, he remains steady and faithful. His strength is exemplified in your weakness, and he will always have more than enough to provide for you.

In which areas of life have you run out of strength? Maybe you're struggling to maintain a good attitude in your relationships. Maybe you're losing the desire to be excellent at your job. Maybe you'd rather not deal with the inconvenience of loving the unlovable. No matter where you've run out of steam, God has what you need. Run to him when you feel like a failure and trust him to provide for you.

Powerful God, thank you for always giving me what I need. Thank you for being my portion and the strength of my heart.

JOY IS COMING

"You will go out with joy and be led out in peace.
The mountains and hills will burst into song before you,
and all the trees in the fields will clap their hands."

Isaiah 55:12 NCV

The promises of God bring joy and peace. They are for your good, and they never fail to exalt the goodness of God's nature. Even when you face trials of many kinds, God assures you that when you trust in him your life will be marked by the good gifts he gives.

As you follow him, you can expect to experience joy and peace. Follow in his footsteps, fill your heart with his Word, and remain hopeful that he will fulfill each of his promises. As you do, he will fill your heart with praise.

Faithful One, I believe that you are still working your promises out in my life and in this earth. You aren't finished moving in miraculous mercy, and your goodness continues to be poured out. I trust you, and I hold onto the hope that joy is coming.

PEACE ALWAYS

The Messiah has come to preach this sweet message of peace to you, the ones who were distant, and to those who are near.

EPHESIANS 2:17 TPT

Christ's message is for everyone, everywhere. The message of his peace and the promise of his salvation are for all who come to him. There is no hierarchy in the kingdom of God, and there are no outcasts.

Christ's message of peace has become your own. Don't save it for when you feel qualified to receive it. As a child of God, your inheritance is secure. Christ's peace belongs to you forever. When life feels stormy, grasp ahold of the goodness of the gospel. Allow the truth of Christ's goodness to permeate your heart and draw your eyes heavenward.

God, I don't want to put limitations on your ability to give me peace. Remind me that I can call on you anytime. Thank you for your goodness that calms my heart.

UNIFIED AND DIGNIFIED

Before me was a great multitude that no one could count, from every nation, tribe, people and language, standing before the throne and before the Lamb. And they cried out in a loud voice: "Salvation belongs to our God."

REVELATION 7:9-10 NIV

At the end of the age, every tribe, nation, language, and people will stand before the throne of God declaring his glory. There will be representatives from every ethnicity on earth. There is unity and dignity for all people in the kingdom of Christ.

Instead of waiting for the fullness of Christ's kingdom to know this type of unity, strive toward it now. Be a messenger of hope who doesn't discriminate against status, ethnicity, race, or class. When you are tempted to ascribe more value to certain people, remember that everyone is worthy of God's love. His desire is to see each of his children redeemed.

Great God, I want to know the power and beauty of knowing you in different expressions, cultures, and friendships. Help me to broaden my horizons and experience you in ways I never knew I could.

PRESENT GOODNESS

If I ride the wings of the morning,
if I dwell by the farthest oceans,
even there your hand will guide me,
and your strength will support me.

PSALM 139:9-10 NLT

The Spirit of God is the fullness of God. The fact that you can never escape from God's Spirit means that you can never escape his goodness. No matter where you go or what you do, God's presence is there. There is great comfort to be found in the Spirit's nearness.

Every moment is an opportunity to lean into the presence of God. The Spirit strengthens you from the inside out, giving you resolve, peace of mind, and courage to persevere through hardships. Whatever you go through today, the presence of God's Spirit is with you. He will give you help for your struggles, strength for your weaknesses, and guidance for each step.

Spirit of God, thank you for being so very accessible. I rely on your strength, grace, and goodness every single day. I love you.

SHINING BRIGHT

The path of the righteous is like the light of dawn,
That shines brighter and brighter until the full day.

PROVERBS 4:18 NASB

As you follow Christ on the pathway of his love, you will walk in the light of his goodness. He lights your way, and you shine brighter and brighter until you come before him in fullness. Even when your life feels dull, the light of God's love can shine brightly still.

May you focus on the one who calls you forward. He shines brighter than the sun, and you reflect his light in your life as you yield to his ways. You can partner with God's purposes as you choose his love, joy, peace, patience, and kindness. Instead of dwelling on life's frustrations or the things you can't change, focus on the glory of God that lights your path.

Jesus, you are source of light, love, and peace. You are my hope in every season of the soul. I choose to continue to follow you. Be glorified in my life.

PEACEFUL HEART

"Peace I leave with you. My peace I give to you. I do not give to you as the world gives. Don't let your heart be troubled or fearful."

JOHN 14:27 CSB

The peace of God is steadfast and sure. It is not given only to be taken away. Do not let your heart be troubled and do not be afraid. There is comfort, peace, and hope to be found in the presence of God. He offers you exactly what you need for today and so much more.

God knows the reality of each of your struggles. He knows what keeps you up at night, and he knows every trial you will face. He knows what your successes will look like, and he knows the full extent of your failures. Even so, he says that his peace is enough for your fears and worries. Grasp ahold of it today and let it permeate your heart.

Faithful God, thank you for inviting me to leave my worries and fears with you. I don't want to be weighed down by them. I choose to give them to you in prayer, and I leave them there. Fill my heart with your peace and calm my mind in your presence.

EVEN MORE GRACE

He gives more grace. Therefore it says, "God opposes the proud but gives grace to the humble."

JAMES 4:6 ESV

The humble heart receives grace upon grace. When you remain open to the Lord's leadership, you will grow in the strength of your faith. God resists the proud, not because they aren't worthy of help, but because they refuse to admit their need of it. When you admit your weaknesses, it allows you to make room for God to move.

There are many ways for you to practically embrace a lifestyle of humility. Try staying quiet and listening when you would rather share your opinion. Try praying for mercy and grace for others rather than correcting them. Readily admit when you are wrong even when it's uncomfortable or even humiliating. God's extensive grace is a treasure that is worth far more than your flesh's desire to be right.

Gracious God, I know that you give grace to the humble, but you resist the proud. I don't want to miss out on the power of your love in my life because I think I already know better.

TREASURES OF DARKNESS

"I will give you the treasures of darkness
and hidden riches of secret places,
that you may know that I, the LORD,
who call you by your name,
am the God of Israel."

ISAIAH 45:3 NKJV

When you walk through the valley of the shadow of death, you have nothing to fear. Even in the darkness, there are treasures to be found. Sometimes you can only see beauty from the other side of a trial but that doesn't mean it wasn't present all along.

Don't resist times of hardship. Even when you can't see them, God's good gifts are everywhere. He will faithfully reveal them to you when the timing is right. He can create sweetness out of the most bitter situations. Turn to him today and trust that he will steadily carry you through whatever you are currently up against.

Lord, I trust you to do what only you can do and bring life to dead things. In the wreckage of my broken dreams, you are still God, and you are still good.

PROMISE KEEPER

Let us hold firmly to the hope that we have confessed, because we can trust God to do what he promised.

HEBREWS 10:23 NCV

Scripture tells you to hold firmly to the hope you've found in Christ. God's steady reminder to be hopeful shows his faithful provision. He knew that you would walk through seasons where hope seems futile. He knew you would want to give up. He knew that some days would seem impossible to endure. Even so, he calls you to hope.

Where have you placed your hope lately? Are you waiting for your finances to look how you want or for your boss to finally see your potential? Are you waiting for a particular relationship to heal or for a phase of life to pass? In all things, Christ is your only reliable source of hope. Look to him and anticipate the fulfillment of God's promises over a shift in your personal circumstances.

Faithful God, I believe that you are the way, the truth, and the life. I believe that you will follow through on every promise you have made. Thank you.

ACCOMPLISHMENTS

God surveyed all he had made and said, "I love it!"
For it pleased him greatly.
Evening gave way to morning— day six.

GENESIS 1:31 TPT

When God was finished creating the world, he looked over everything. When he took it in, he couldn't help but be pleased with what he found. He loved it! He was delighted by every facet of creation. He surveyed each part and declared how good it was.

May you find the same delight as you look over your own accomplishments and creative endeavors. It is good to take time to survey what you've done. It's okay to find pleasure in the things you are proud of. You don't need to rush on to the next thing or move forward in a strictly productive manner. Take a moment and look over your work with humility and gratitude.

Creator, thank you for making me with intention and creativity. I want to delight in the things I put my hands to in the same way that you do. Help me take time to appreciate my work.

SING YOUR GRATITUDE

Let the message of Christ dwell among you richly as you teach and admonish one another with all wisdom through psalms, hymns, and songs from the Spirit, singing to God with gratitude in your hearts.

COLOSSIANS 3:16 NIV

Scripture is filled with examples of people using music to offer their praise to the Lord. In the Psalms there are many different expressions and poetic songs that were used in the tabernacle of the Lord. Even Paul writes that we should encourage each other through song.

No matter what your personal preference or style is, it's difficult to deny the power of music. Music can express truth in a way that is impactful and meaningful. It can speak to your soul in a way that spoken words can't. There is beauty and strength in offering a sacrifice of praise to God. Connect with God in this way and let your heart be encouraged.

Worthy One, I want to connect with you through music today. Move in my heart as I offer songs to you. I love you.

STEP OF FAITH

It was by faith that Abraham obeyed when God called him to leave home and go to another land that God would give him as his inheritance. He went without knowing where he was going.

Hebrews 11:8 NLT

When God called Abraham to leave everything he knew and follow him into the great unknown, Abraham had no idea where he would end up. He didn't have a ten-step plan of how to get from where he was to where he felt like God was calling him to go. He simply obeyed and took the first step. As he was on his way, God directed him.

Have you been putting off making the first move of faith for fear of the unknown? Trust that God will guide you, just as he did with Abraham. He goes with you, and he will direct you. You don't need to know every detail. There is nothing to fear when you walk with God who is infinitely faithful.

Good God, I trust you to guide me into your goodness, even though I don't know how things will turn out. Settle my heart with your peace and help me to take each step you reveal to me.

SEPTEMBER

Your word is a lamp for my feet
and a light on my path.

Psalm 119:105 CSB

REASONS TO TRUST

"Behold, God is my salvation,
I will trust and not be afraid;
For the LORD God is my strength and my song,
And He has become my salvation."

ISAIAH 12:2 NASB

Christ is your salvation. He has done everything needed so that you can freely come to him, experience redemption and forgiveness, and live liberated in his lavish love. Nothing keeps you from fellowship with God when you come through Christ.

Through Christ, you have access to everything you need. As you turn to him today, allow him to meet your needs. Bring him your concerns, worries, and fears. He is your competent help, gracious comforter, and powerful defender. Meet with him and trust him with your life.

Lord, I believe you are completely unfailing in love. Your mercy is powerful to save, and I don't have to earn it. I am grateful for how you have helped me, and I am convinced that you will continue to.

LIVING WATER

"Whoever drinks the water I give will never be thirsty. The water I give will become a spring of water gushing up inside that person, giving eternal life."

JOHN 4:14 CSB

Jesus offers you living water that satisfies your soul. It is water that does not just quench your thirst but also produces gushing fountains of life within you. You can experience inner refreshment at all times because of the life that Christ infuses in you through the Spirit. Eternal life is available to you each and every day.

Come to the presence of God and drink deeply from his refreshing waters. Let him revive your soul. Ask him and he will give you clarity, energy, and strength to face whatever comes your way. The fountain of God's presence is unending, and you can drink from it at any moment, no matter where you are.

Holy Spirit, I don't want to neglect your power in my life. Fill me afresh with the powerful living water you offer. Thank you.

CORDS OF KINDNESS

"I led them with cords of kindness, with the bands of love, and I became to them as one who eases the yoke on their jaws, and I bent down to them and fed them."

Hosea 11:4 ESV

God does not enslave you. You are not bound to him by obligation or an imbalance of power. You committed your life to him, and he has committed to leading you with kindness and love. If anything, the scales are outweighed in your favor. If you ever feel stuck, trapped, or bitter about the way he asks you to live, remember the immense freedom he has offered you.

Sometimes when you've followed the Lord for a long time, parts of your life can begin to feel mundane or obligatory. You might go through the motions because you're so accustomed to living a certain way. Today, fight against the tendency to glaze over the miracle of salvation. God has done everything for you, and he has done it with kindness, gentleness, and immense care.

Merciful One, thank you for your unrelenting kindness toward me. I am grateful that even in suffering, you are near, lifting the weight of my burdens. I lean on you, trusting that my breakthrough is coming.

LISTEN FOR IT

"My sheep hear My voice, and I know them,
and they follow Me."

JOHN 10:27 NKJV

A sheep follows its shepherd with confidence because it is convinced of his ability to provide. A sheep listens when the shepherd speaks because it knows it depends on the shepherd for survival. God wants you to know him in the same way. He wants you to recognize his voice in all circumstances.

Recognizing God's voice can only happen if you take the time to get to know him. Saturate your life with the Word. Search Scripture and get to know his character. The more you know about him the more confident you will be about the way he moves. Draw near to him today and increase your understanding of your good Shepherd.

Good Shepherd, thank you for being accessible and near today. Speak to me, and bring life, hope, and clarity to my heart and mind as you do. I want to know you more.

HEART DETECTION

"These people show honor to me with words, but their hearts are far from me."

MARK 7:6 NCV

Jesus knew the hearts of the religious scholars who challenged the way that he and his disciples lived. The Pharisees and religious leaders thought Jesus' disciples were not following the letter of the law, but Jesus called them out on their hypocrisy. Their hearts were far from God even though their outward lives appeared to be spotless.

Remain humble before God because he cannot be manipulated or fooled. Your greatest success doesn't impress him, and your most proficient skills don't sway his opinion of you. He looks at your heart and examines the depths of who you are. You can offer him your whole heart and trust him to transform it into his likeness. Draw near to him today and remember that your relationship with him matters more than anything you do or don't do.

Lord, I humble my heart before you. Draw me closer to you and fill me with your love. Help me prioritize my relationship with you above all else.

EVERY DETAIL

Tell him every detail of your life, then God's wonderful peace that transcends human understanding, will guard your heart and mind through Jesus Christ.

PHILIPPIANS 4:6-7 TPT

You don't have to hide a single detail of your life from God. He wants in on all of it. It's not frivolous to talk to him as a friend. In fact, your fellowship with his Spirit will grow even deeper as you include him in the trivial things and the more substantial parts of your life.

Have you ever felt like what you felt didn't matter to anyone else? Well, it matters to God. He promises to give you peace when you share your life with him. As you deepen your friendship with him, you will find yourself even more convinced of his faithfulness.

Lord, what a liberating idea it is that you are interested in every detail of my life. I want to know you as a friend. Reveal your nearness and love as I talk to you throughout my day and pour out my heart to you.

BEGINNING AND END

"I am the Alpha and the Omega," says the Lord God, "who is, and who was, and who is to come, the Almighty."

REVELATION 1:8 NIV

God the Almighty is above all. He is outside the limits of our understanding. He was at the beginning, and he will be present at the end of all things. He is with you now through his Spirit, and he won't ever leave you.

In light of God's vastness, how small do your problems seem? This is not to say that they are insignificant. He cares intimately about your concerns, but he is not worried about your worries. He is not swayed by the things that trouble you. He is steady, faithful, and able to see you through it all. May your heart hide in his goodness and may your mind rest in his peace.

Everlasting God, I cannot truly comprehend how great you are, but I trust that you are bigger and better than I can imagine. I am overwhelmed by your kindness.

HE ALREADY KNOWS

"Your Father knows exactly what you need even before you ask him!"

MATTHEW 6:8 NLT

God knows your needs before you bring them up. May this truth bring comfort and relief to your heart as you trust him with your life today. He knows what you don't even know to ask for. Trust that he will provide what you need.

It can feel startling when unexpected crises arise. You can't always anticipate problems, but God knows exactly what the trajectory of your life is. He knows every obstacle you will come across, and he has the solutions for every problem you face. He is always near and eager to provide for you.

Almighty God, you already know what I need today, and I trust you to provide my daily bread. I choose to walk in your ways. May your kingdom come, and your will be done on earth, as it is in heaven.

IN JESUS' NAME

Whatever you do in word or deed, do everything in the name of the Lord Jesus, giving thanks through Him to God the Father.

COLOSSIANS 3:17 NASB

Each day is an opportunity to offer your life to God in an act of worship. When you give him the details of your day, the demanding voices of the world will fade away. You can choose to do all things for the audience of your beloved Savior alone.

There isn't a scale of appropriate sacrifices to give to God. He doesn't rank your service from big to small. All things are acceptable to be given to him. From the way you speak to others to the attitude you have at work, each part of your life can be a sacrifice unto him. Don't try to compartmentalize your faith into stereotypical religious acts. Instead, offer every part of your life to the Lord.

Father, thank you for each opportunity to serve and honor you. Help me see each part of my life as worthy to offer you in worship.

LEAN ON HIS HELP

"Be strong and courageous, and do the work. Don't be afraid or discouraged, for the LORD God, my God, is with you. He won't leave you or abandon you until all the work for the service of the LORD's house is finished."

1 CHRONICLES 28:20 CSB

No matter what your work looks like, you can confidently know that God is with you through it all. He will not leave you to figure it out on your own, and he will not forsake you in our time of need. As you stand upon that truth, you can move forward with strength and courage.

God asks you to have courage because he is fully capable of backing you up. He doesn't ask you to be strong on your own. He asks you to lean on his strength and faithfully do what he's called you to do. Acknowledge him and he will fully equip you to steadily work according to his will.

Lord, thank you for your help as I do the work you have called me to do. I need you every single day. When I am weak, you are my strength.

CLARITY OF MIND

God is not a God of confusion but of peace.

1 Corinthians 14:33 ESV

God never operates in confusion. Everything he does is based in love, peace, grace, and mercy. He does not turn you around in circles or have unreasonable expectations. Rather, he straightens your path and gives you wisdom whenever you ask. He brings clarity to your confusion and peace to your anxiety.

If you are confused in any area of your life, ask God to give you his peace. The world is a confusing place, but God's presence is not. It is full of light, love, peace, joy, and hope. It is not a place of intimidation, control, or secrecy. God's wisdom is simple, straight-forward, and always rooted in love.

Wise God, speak the simplicity of your truth over my circumstances today. I don't want to be caught up in a web of confusion that you never designed for me. I'm thankful for your wisdom, and I trust you.

OBEDIENT DEVOTION

The fear of the LORD is the beginning of knowledge,
but fools despise wisdom and instruction.

PROVERBS 1:7 NKJV

The essence of wisdom is found in the Lord. When you live in obedient devotion to God and his ways, you admit that you don't know best. You can follow His directions because your heart is open to his correction and redirection.

When you resist admitting when you are wrong, you refuse to leave room for the weakness of your humanity. Don't close yourself off from learning and growing. If you already think you know everything there is to know, every failure will feel catastrophic. Open your heart and be willing to adjust when your life doesn't align with God's will.

Lord, you are full of wisdom. I don't want to walk in conceit or pride, but in love and humility. I honor you and your nature above all things.

JOYFUL HOPE

Be joyful because you have hope. Be patient when trouble comes, and pray at all times.

ROMANS 12:12 NCV

Hope is not simply an ideal or some intangible thing you talk about. As a believer, hope is found through fellowship with the Holy Spirit. As you commune with him, he reminds you of the truth. He encourages you trust in Jesus no matter what happens.

Even if the circumstances of your life don't seem joyful, you can know the pure joy of the Lord in the midst of them. As you pray today, offer God whatever you have. No matter how meagre your sacrifice seems, he will take it and offer you the comfort and peace of his presence.

Holy Spirit, you infuse me with hope in the depths of my soul. Thank you for ministering to me on all occasions. You know exactly what I need today. Fill me with the good fruit of your presence.

TIMELY REMINDERS

Remind them to never tear down anyone with their words or quarrel, but instead be considerate, humble, and courteous to everyone.

Titus 3:2 TPT

When you are on the defensive, it is natural to want to return harsh words with cutting ones. What comes naturally is not always the best way to deal with others. Jesus instructs you to love in all circumstances. While it's not easy, it is God honoring when you love people who are difficult to love.

When others are looking for a fight, you don't have to participate. You can maintain the peace of your own heart and refuse to be hooked by their advances. Take time to pray and God will equip you to have self-control and patience. As you seek to honor him, he will help you stay grounded in love.

Lord, help me to remain rooted in your love in all my interactions today. When I'm tempted to use my words as weapons, help me to instead to use them as a salve.

SUSTAINED BY THE LORD

I lie down and sleep;
I wake again, because the Lord sustains me.

Psalm 3:5 NIV

Before you move on with your day, no matter what has already happened or what is looming over you, take some time to meditate on today's verse. You are here because God has given you another day. Every moment is an opportunity to choose how you want to engage in this gift of life.

Your life is not a mistake, and you are not here by accident. You were created by a thoughtful God who delights in you. There is so much mercy for you today. He has so much to share with you. Will you spend time in his presence, letting him speak his words of life over you? You are here, and he wants you to know him in deeper ways.

Sustainer, you are the giver of life, and you are my creator. Thank you for the gift of today. Show me how to use the time you've given me.

LOOSEN YOUR GRIP

"If you try to hang on to your life, you will lose it. But if you give up your life for my sake, you will save it."

MATTHEW 16:25 NLT

You probably have an idea of what you think your life should look like. You make plans according to your expectations and move forward as best you can. It's good to work toward a goal, but problems occur when you put too much weight on your own ideas.

Having a firm grip on your plans will lead to disappointment. Hold your expectations with a loose grasp and trust God to lead you. If your eyes are steadily turned toward him, you won't be as focused on the ups and downs of life. He knows what you need, and you can trust him to guide you. Take a deep breath and surrender to the author and perfecter of your faith.

Jesus Christ, I don't want to hold so tightly to my plans for this life that I refuse to allow your mercy any room to redeem and restore what is broken. I choose to follow you, for you are wonderful, trustworthy, and true.

AUTHORITY

All who are being led by the Spirit of God, these are sons of God. For you have not received a spirit of slavery leading to fear again, but you have received a spirit of adoption as sons by which we cry out, "Abba! Father!"

ROMANS 8:14-15 NASB

You have been adopted into the family of God. He has given you a new name, and you belong with him. God is not just a sovereign leader, but he is your kind and gracious Father. He loves you like a good father loves his children.

You have been welcomed into God's kingdom by Jesus. As a result, God shares everything he has with you. You are part of his family, and he doesn't hold back. He is generous and attentive, and he is delighted to call you his own. Run to him as a child runs to their father and fully expect him to be overjoyed to see you.

Abba, you are my Father, and I am your child. Lead me in your love and reveal the power of your authority in my life. Continue to teach me your ways as I follow you.

PRESS ON

Not that I have already reached the goal or am already perfect, but I make every effort to take hold of it because I also have been taken hold of by Christ Jesus.

PHILIPPIANS 3:12 CSB

You are a work in progress, and you have not run out of time. Don't fret if your life doesn't look the way you hoped. No matter how old you are, God is still working on your behalf. As long as you have breath in your lungs, your story isn't over.

God's concept of time is not the same as yours. While you might be discouraged that certain things haven't happened, God is not dismayed. He knows what your life will look like. Instead of panicking over the details, put your life in the hands of the one who knows best. Trust him with the parts of your life you don't understand and press on toward what's next.

Lord Jesus, knowing you completely is the goal of my faith. I don't want to get tripped up or distracted by things that don't matter. I press on to know you more.

SIMPLE WILL

He has told you, O man, what is good,
and what does the LORD require of you
but to do justice, and to love kindness,
and to walk humbly with your God.

MICAH 6:8 ESV

God's will is not a mystery. It is not some vague thing to grasp or try to figure out. What does the Lord require of you? As it says in today's verse, do justice, love kindness, and walk humbly with your God. The implications of these things may be different for everyone, but the foundation is the same.

Your character matters more than the things you accomplish. You will do a great many things in life but the way you do them is what's most important. If you want to honor the Lord, focus on loving justice, treating others kindly, and being humble in his presence. Instead of agonizing over what job to take or where to live, remember you can implement God's desires for you into every set of circumstances.

God, thank you for the power of your wisdom and the simplicity of your truth. Help me practically apply your Word to my life. May I honor you in all I do.

WALKING ON WATER

He said, "Come." And when Peter had come down out of the boat, he walked on the water to go to Jesus.

MATTHEW 14:29 NKJV

All the disciples were in the boat with Peter when Jesus invited him to walk on the water. Have you ever wondered why no one else was asked to join him outside of the boat? Back up one verse and you will see. When the disciples first spotted Jesus on the water, they thought he was a ghost. Jesus sought to calm their fears by reassuring them. Peter asked Jesus to invite him to walk among the waves.

Peter wanted to walk on the water with Jesus, and Jesus honored his desire. This did not make him any better or worse than the disciples who remained on the boat. When you have a desire in your heart, reach out to the Lord with it. He may invite you into a place of miracles where he will keep you afloat if your eyes are on him.

Jesus, thank you for responding to my requests. Thank you for calling me closer to you all the time. You are so wonderful. May my faith grow stronger.

BELIEVE HIM

Jesus paid no attention to what they said. He told the synagogue leader, "Don't be afraid; just believe."

MARK 5:36 NCV

In today's Scripture Jairus had just been notified that his daughter had died while they were still on their way to his home. This is the context of Jesus' command to set aside fear and believe. The circumstances were devastating, and he still called Jairus to trust him.

With God, all things are possible. Dead things come to life, old dreams are resurrected, and miracles happen. When Jesus compels you to trust him, do it. He will not let you down. He is able to do far more than you can imagine. You can trust him even when reality is grim, and you can't see a way forward.

God, I believe you over even the harsh realities I face. You are faithful, and I trust you to guide me with your love. Display your power in my life as I choose to take you at your Word.

TAKEN CARE OF

"People everywhere seem to worry about making a living, but your heavenly Father knows your every need and will take care of you."

LUKE 12:30 TPT

Have the pressures of life weighed you down? Perhaps you feel stuck in cycles of lack, uncertainty, and indecision. Even when you have no idea how you will meet a need, your heavenly Father knows how. He will take care of you.

Sometimes God will change your circumstances, and sometimes he will change your heart. You don't have to worry either way. He is perfectly capable of giving you exactly what you need. If you have committed a situation to him, you can trust that he is handling it exactly the right way. Today, give him your worries and don't pick them up again.

Heavenly Father, I want my trust in your faithfulness to grow deeper. I know this happens through experience, relationship, and walking with you. I don't want to worry about making a living. I choose to trust your goodness and provision.

RESTORED BY GOD

"Let their flesh be renewed like a child's;
let them be restored as in the days of their youth
then that person can pray to God and find favor with him,
they will see God's face and shout for joy;
he will restore them to full well-being."

JOB 33:25-26 NIV

Job lost everything. He lost his health, material possessions, and family. Even though he suffered great losses, he did not lose his faith. Even when his friends encouraged him to give up hope, he could not. In the depths of his grief and questioning, God did not abandon him. He will not abandon you either.

God restores what tragedy steals, and he brings beauty out of the ashes of defeat. If you find yourself in a season of suffering, do not give up hope. Just as surely as the sun rises each morning and sets in the evening, so will God see you through. He can guide you through the dark and bring relief when you need it most.

Lord, thank you for the power of your restoration. Do it again, Lord, and revive my heart and life in your love.

HEALING IN CONFESSION

Confess your sins to each other and pray for each other so that you may be healed. The earnest prayer of a righteous person has great power and produces wonderful results.

JAMES 5:16 NLT

It can be incredibly healing to share a confession with someone trustworthy. The weight of your sin is too heavy for you to carry alone. When you willingly share your failures, your burden is lightened. When you are vulnerable about your mistakes, other people feel the freedom to do the same.

It is good to humbly admit your failures and ask for encouragement. You aren't meant to live a God honoring life all alone. You need the perspectives, accountability, and help of other believers. Find a friend who is reliable and spur each other on toward godliness.

Righteous One, I don't want to hide things that need to be brought to the light, but I also don't want to be foolish about who I confess these things to. Give me wisdom to know who is trustworthy and true. Thank you.

GROWING UP IN GOD

Leaving the elementary teaching about the Christ, let us press on to maturity, not laying again a foundation of repentance from dead works and of faith toward God, of instruction about washings and laying on of hands, and the resurrection of the dead and eternal judgment.

HEBREWS 6:1-2 NASB

If you find yourself continuously repenting out of guilt and shame, you might be caught in a cycle of insecurity. While it's good to be aware of your mistakes, Jesus has already paid the price for your sins. He wants you to run to him with confidence rather than shame.

When you make mistakes, you don't need to hide or sheepishly ask for help. Go to him boldly and expect him to be merciful because he says he will be. Don't doubt his character when he has assured you that it will never change. As you mature in your faith, your ability to trust God will increase. The more you experience his love, the more you'll be confident of his redemption.

Father, help me grow in confidence of your mercy. Teach me about your character and remind me of the truth when I waver. Thank you for walking me along a path toward wholeness.

DON'T GIVE UP

Let us not get tired of doing good, for we will reap at the proper time if we don't give up.

GALATIANS 6:9 CSB

God wouldn't warn you not to get tired of doing good if he didn't think you never would. He knew you would have days when it feels impossible to move forward. He knew you would grow weary of doing the same things over and over. He knew that following him would come with a level of sacrifice.

Be encouraged that you are not alone in your weariness. Everyone wants to give up sometimes. The difference is whether or not you lean on the Lord for fortitude. He will strengthen you when you are weary. He will encourage you when you are tired of the work you are doing. Don't give up on what God has asked you to do. If you don't quit, you win.

Righteous One, give me the gift of fortitude today. I don't want to quit when things get hard. Help me persevere in doing good as I look to you for strength.

CHRIST OUR HEAD

Speaking the truth in love, we are to grow up in every way into him who is the head, into Christ, from whom the whole body, joined and held together by every joint with which it is equipped, when each part is working properly, makes the body grow so that it builds itself up in love.

EPHESIANS 4:15-16 ESV

You have a specific part to play in the body of Christ. God created you with creativity and intentionality. Your gifts might look different from the people around you, but they aren't any more or less valuable.

Remember that when you embrace your role, the whole body thrives. In the same way, rejoice when others flourish in how God made them. Their success is your success. Don't give in to the temptation to compare yourself to others. Instead, stay in your lane and cheer on the people around you.

Christ, I am grateful for who I am in you. Help me to serve others in love and do my part well. May I mature in your truth and leave room for the gifts and strengths of others.

UNSHAKEABLE TRUST

The king was overjoyed and gave orders to take Daniel out of the den. When Daniel was brought up from the den, he was found to be unharmed, for he trusted in his God.

DANIEL 6:23 CSB

The story of Daniel in the lion's den is a miraculous one. God shut the mouths of the lions and kept Daniel from harm. Daniel relied on God's strength when he was at his weakest point. Even though his situation seemed impossible, he did not waver.

Your connection with God is your lifeline. Through him you have access to his power, provision, grace, and mercy. He has everything you could ever need. Having a relationship with him is the greatest gift you could ever be given. If he showed up for Daniel, he will show up for you. Don't give up pursuing the God who rescues his children from the lion's den.

My God, I love that you are powerful beyond measure and overwhelming in kindness toward your children. I trust you as you continue to reveal yourself to me.

CHOOSING FORGIVENESS

Bear with each other, and forgive each other. If someone does wrong to you, forgive that person because the Lord forgave you.

COLOSSIANS 3:13 NCV

It is not always easy to choose to forgiveness. In fact, it's usually downright painful. God asks you to trust him even with wounds that seem impossible or fatal. However, he doesn't ask you to heal your wounds alone. He offers you grace and mercy as you trust in him.

Forgiveness can take time, but it also takes intention. There won't be many times you feel like forgiving others. It's much more comfortable to insist on your way and hold your ground. While you might feel vindicated, that isn't the way of Christ. Humbly lay your weapons down, and trust that God knows what is best. He will empower you to forgive when it is beyond your ability.

Merciful Father, thank you for your grace. I don't want to become bitter with unforgiveness. Help me to trust you and truly forgive those who hurt me.

FOUND IN HIM

It is through him that we live and function and have our identity; just as your own poets have said, "Our lineage comes from him."

ACTS 17:28 TPT

In Christ you live, move, and have your being. Your existence stems directly from him. In other words, without him, you would be hopeless and lost. Everything you are and have comes from him. When you recognize that he is interwoven into every part of your existence, faith feels more like second nature than something to attain.

Deliberately turn away from the tendency to compartmentalize your faith. God cannot be contained to the areas of your life you think he belongs in. He is fully part of everything. His presence is as close as the air you breathe. He is your Father, and you are found in him.

Good Father, in you I live and function and have my very identity. I am your child, and you are my good Father. Be honored and glorified in every part of my life.

OCTOBER

Draw near to God,
and he will draw near to you.

JAMES 4:8 CSB

HELP ME BELIEVE

Immediately the boy's father exclaimed, "I do believe; help me overcome my unbelief!"

MARK 9:24 NIV

God is not intimidated by your doubts. In fact, when you are honest about your lack of faith in certain areas, it leaves room for God to move. When you readily admit your doubts, you can also acknowledge that God is the only one who can adjust the way you think.

God can move in your life despite your doubts. He is not limited by your faulty or flawed thought patterns. He knows that sometimes it is hard to maintain faith. Trust him to guide you even when you are unsure. Give him your questions and believe that he knows what to do with them. As you place your hesitations in his hands, he will strengthen your faith bit by bit. He is your ever-present help in times of need even when you are struggling with unbelief.

Miracle Worker, I know that everything is possible for you and for those who believe. Increase my faith as I continue to walk in your ways. I believe that you can do the impossible. Help my unbelief!

ASKED AND GRANTED

The LORD grants wisdom!
From his mouth come knowledge and understanding.

PROVERBS 2:6 NLT

God offers wisdom to all who earnestly search for it. As long as you are open to correction and looking for insight, God will grant it to you. He does not expect you to have all of the answers. Dependence on God's wisdom shows more spiritual maturity than insisting you have it all figured out.

You don't have to wonder if God will help you. He promises to do it whenever you ask. He longs to partner with you in every part of your life. He cares about seemingly insignificant details and life-changing decisions. In all things, lean on the knowledge and understanding of the Lord.

Lord, I trust you to give me wisdom and direction. I will rest in the peace of your presence as I wait on your reply. Thank you.

KINGDOM ATTRIBUTES

The kingdom of God is not eating and drinking, but righteousness and peace and joy in the Holy Spirit.

ROMANS 14:17 NASB

The kingdom of God is not made up of rules and regulations. It is not about what you eat, how you dress, or any other outward expression. The kingdom of God is defined by the fruit of his Spirit. Love, patience, kindness, goodness, peace, joy, self-control, faithfulness, and gentleness matter most.

You can't cultivate the fruit of the Spirit without the presence of the Spirit. As you follow him, he will help manifest those things in your life. Instead of getting caught up in rules or particulars that don't matter, focus on the character God has asked you to display.

Great God, may the fruit of your kingdom be apparent in my life as I partner with your purposes. Keep my eyes on you and help me focus on what really matters. Keep me from being distracted by the ways of the world.

NOURISHING GRACE

I commit you to God and to the word of his grace, which is able to build you up and to give you an inheritance among all who are sanctified.

ACTS 20:32 CSB

God's grace is what empowers you to live a life that is defined by his love. By his grace you can turn to him in obedience. By his grace your heart stays soft to his instruction. By his grace you are filled with the Holy Spirit and empowered to do what is right.

When you have a clear picture of grace, you will be strengthened and encouraged. God's grace is what gives you the ability to follow him. His undeserved love and forgiveness are what give you courage and hope. Feast on the grace of God today as you spend time in his presence.

Generous Father, thank you for your grace and the power of it in my life. I believe that it is all I need today. Strengthen me in the areas I am weak and continue to build me up in the truth of who you are. Thank you.

POWER OF SCRIPTURE

All Scripture is breathed out by God and profitable for teaching, for reproof, for correction, and for training in righteousness, that the man of God may be complete, equipped for every good work.

2 TIMOTHY 3:16-17 ESV

Every word within Scripture is powerful and intentional. Through Scripture you can see a clear picture of your humanity and the unrelenting mercy of God woven into every story. There is wisdom for the reality of your life, and there is encouragement for the journey ahead.

Today, ask God for a fresh revelation of Scripture. Ask him for greater understanding as you read through it. He will make his ways clear to you. If your heart is soft, he won't leave you empty handed. Approach the Word with curious eyes and an attitude of expectation.

Righteous One, thank you for revealing your character through Scripture. Teach me more about you today as I delve into your Word.

ROOM FOR WEAKNESS

I take pleasure in infirmities, in reproaches, in needs, in persecutions, in distresses, for Christ's sake. For when I am weak, then I am strong.

2 CORINTHIANS 12:10 NKJV

It might seem foolish to take pleasure in the hardest areas of your life. It's certainly counterintuitive. Your natural reaction isn't usually to rejoice in times of suffering. This is why you need the wisdom of the Holy Spirit. He is the one who empowers you despite your weakness.

Joy through sorrow doesn't mean you have to be irrationally happy. It doesn't mean you have to ignore trials or water down the difficulties in your life. Joy through sorrow means that you are able to recognize the opportunity that weakness brings. Through weakness, God's strength is ever more amplified. Through weakness, you are able to depend on him even more than usual.

Gracious God, thank you for the empowering grace of your presence that meets me in my weakness. I want to learn, as Paul did, to delight in suffering. Teach me, refine me, and increase my understanding of your love as you carry me through hardship.

HIS KINDNESS

I will tell about the LORD's kindness
and praise him for everything he has done.
He has shown great mercy to us
and has been very kind to us.

ISAIAH 63:7 NCV

How have you seen God's mercy and kindness displayed in your own life? Every fulfilled need and answered prayer is a story to tell. He has shown up in your life in big and small ways. He has faithfully carried you this far, and it can be encouraging to recognize how he has done it.

Take time today to recount God's faithfulness in your life. Ask the Holy Spirit to remind you how he cared for you. As you remember, be strengthened by God's steadiness and consistency. Let your faith be strengthened by what God has already done and let it stir up hope for the future.

Kind God, thank you for your goodness toward me. Help me remember all that you've done for me. Bring to mind your faithfulness and give me hope for the future.

FROM WORRY TO FAITH

"Don't worry or surrender to your fear. For you've believed in God, now trust and believe in me also."

JOHN 14:1 TPT

Jesus' invitation to you today is to lay down your fear and worry. Don't give into the anxieties that flood your heart and mind. Instead, offer them to God. As you do, believe that he will take care of you, for he promises to do so.

What are the worries and fears that threaten your peace? What are the things you have not been able to shake off? Ignoring them won't fix the weight of their existence. However, offering them to Christ in exchange for his perfect peace is just what you need.

Faithful One, I choose to give you every worry and anxiety on my heart and in my mind today. I won't stop until they're all laid out before you. I choose to believe that you will take care of them.

DAILY SURRENDER

He said to them all: "Whoever wants to be my disciple must deny themselves and take up their cross daily and follow me."

LUKE 9:23 NIV

Following Jesus is so much more than practicing the religion of your parents or grandparents. It's so much more than trying to do the right thing or striving to maintain a list of rules. Following Jesus isn't about ideology. It's about laying down your life and choosing his way over your own.

Daily surrender to the Lord and his leadership is the epitome of your faith. You can't follow Jesus without some element of self-denial. This means that you acknowledge that his ways are higher than your own, and you humbly surrender yourself to his lordship. It means that no matter what comes your way, you rely upon the gentle kingship of Jesus.

Lord, I surrender to your will and ways today. I choose to follow you, and I know that requires denial of opposing values. I offer you my life, and I trust you to lead me in truth.

IDENTIFIABLE FRUIT

"Just as you can identify a tree by its fruit, so you can identify people by their actions."

MATTHEW 7:20 NLT

If your actions don't line up with your words, there is a discrepancy in your faith. If you say you follow Jesus but don't honor his instructions, then you've missed the point. When you encounter God's love and apply his truth to your life, you will have obvious fruit.

Even if you examine your life and don't see any godly fruit, it isn't too late. It is always the right time to turn to the Lord. Don't let your failures or shortcomings cause shame to dominate your thinking. Instead, humbly turn to God and let him mercifully draw you back to his heart.

Wise God, I humble myself before you. Show me areas of my life that aren't producing fruit. I submit to your ways, and I trust your leadership. I trust you to cultivate your love in my life.

FIRST THING

In the morning, LORD, You will hear my voice;
In the morning I will present my prayer to You and be on the watch.

PSALM 5:3 NASB

You probably know that healthy habits and practices are good for you. Drinking enough water is good for your body. Getting fresh air each day is good for your soul. Talking to God each morning is life-giving for your spirit. The habit of prayer is a sweet gift not an obligation or something you should feel ashamed for not doing.

Turn toward God each morning. Tell him about your hopes for the day and ask for what you need. Acknowledge who he is and say thank you for the blessings in your life. As you start your day with him, he will give you peace and strength to face whatever is coming your way.

Ever-Present One, I'm so grateful for your nearness every moment of every day. As I train my heart and mind to connect with you first thing in the morning, refresh me with your words of life.

LEARNING OPPORTUNITIES

It was good for me to be afflicted
so that I could learn your statutes.

Psalm 119:71 CSB

If you've ever wallowed in self-defamation or pity after a failure, you know that doesn't lead to anything good. There is no fruit to be found in beating yourself up or being your own worst critic. Instead of embracing failure as an indication of your worth, ask God to help you shift your perspective.

Every failure is simply an opportunity to learn more about God. As you embrace your weakness, God's strength is magnified. As you recognize your shortcomings, he has an even greater chance to show you his faithfulness. Let your weakness point you to the only one who can lift you up.

Great God, learning to let go of perfectionism and pride is one of the hardest parts about growing into maturity. Help me humbly admit my wrongs and confidently trust you for healing.

NO ACCUSATIONS

There is therefore now no condemnation for those who are in Christ Jesus.

ROMANS 8:1 ESV

If you have chosen to follow Jesus, freedom is yours for the taking. You are no longer bound to the weight of sin and death. He has taken your burdens upon himself. When you notice yourself trying to take them back from him, remind yourself of the sufficiency of the cross. Christ's death and resurrection are more than enough to secure your eternal freedom.

Freedom is yours no matter where accusations come from. The opinions of others cannot diminish what Christ has done for you. If you are your own worst critic, you might be guilty of holding yourself to an impossible standard. Stop striving and rest in the truth that Jesus has done all the work for you.

Redeemer, thank you for the power of your sacrifice over sin, death, fear, and shame. You are better than life itself, and you are my soul's liberation. Thank you for setting me free and giving me an abundance of mercy and grace.

GREATER THAN ANY ARMY

"This is the word of the LORD to Zerubbabel:
'Not by might nor by power, but by My Spirit,'
says the LORD of hosts."

ZECHARIAH 4:6 NKJV

Nothing is impossible for God. By his Spirit, mountains are moved, the sick are healed, and the dead are raised. The resurrection power of Christ's life is greater than any show of force in this world.

When you look at the state of the world, are you discouraged? Instead of feeling hopeless about what's going on, look to the one who created the heavens and the earth. Align your heart in the great power of God's love today. He has not stopped moving. Trust him and look for the move of his Spirit.

Spirit of God, move in the world to bring peace, clarity, and justice. We all need your hand upon our lives. Open my eyes to see how you are moving.

DWELLING PLACE

Don't you know that you are God's temple and that God's Spirit lives in you?

1 Corinthians 3:16 NCV

You don't have to wait to find God in a sacred place or religious setting. You are God's temple. The Spirit of God makes his home in you. Wherever you are, if you are in Christ, then the sacred place of meeting is inside of you.

Take a moment right now to close your eyes and turn your attention to your heart. God dwells in the depths of you. If you are Christ's, then you are home in him, and he is at home in you. You don't lack anything today, for you have the fullness of God's Spirit within you. Meditate on that as you commune with him, spirit to Spirit.

Lord God, thank you that I don't have to go anywhere to meet with you. Thank you for dwelling within me. Thank you for your constant help and companionship.

MORE THAN A THEORY

Beloved children, our love can't be an abstract theory we only talk about, but a way of life demonstrated through our loving deeds.

1 John 3:18 TPT

If the love of God is only something you talk about, you miss out on its true power. The love of God is a force. An active pursuit of God's love is defined by service to one another. If you talk about how much you love God and yet don't have any loving deeds to point to, then your words are empty.

Let God's love filter through your heart and impact everything you do. Be motivated, encouraged, and empowered by his love. When you come up short, turn to him for a fresh revelation. When you can't go another step, depend on his strength to love over your own. He calls you to love in practical ways, and he equips you to do it.

Lord, I'm so grateful that your love is an active force, not just a theory or idea. I choose to follow you by being practical in kindness, mercy, and love. I follow your example.

COVENANT OF PEACE

"Though the mountains be shaken
and the hills be removed,
yet my unfailing love for you will not be shaken
nor my covenant of peace be removed,"
says the LORD, who has compassion on you.

ISAIAH 54:10 NIV

Even when the chaos of the world heightens, the covenant of God's peace is unshakeable. It remains steadfast and true. God does what he promises. He is faithful in all ways, at all times, and to all who trust in him. When you see wickedness rising, remember that God's love will overpower it in the end.

God's presence brings peace to your inner world, even when your outer world is turned upside-down. Meditate on God's unfailing love. If you follow him, you are promised to see his goodness while you are living. May you know the confidence of his faithfulness toward you, for he never fails.

Powerful One, thank you for the reminder that no matter what is going on in my life or in the world, you are bigger still. You are full of unfailing love, resurrection power, and incomparable wisdom. You will never fail, and I choose to trust you.

PROMISE OF PRESENCE

"I will be with you as I was with Moses. I will not fail you or abandon you. Be strong and courageous."

JOSHUA 1:5-6 NLT

Have you ever felt as if God was too far away? Feelings of loneliness or abandonment can lead you to doubt God's goodness. As you mature, you'll learn to lean on the truth rather you're your feelings. Though you may feel far from God, you know he is close. Though you may feel alone, you know he has promised to be with you at all times.

Moses is known as a father of the faith, and you have the same access to God that he had. You even have the indwelling of the Holy Spirit to guide you every moment of the day. This is almost too much to comprehend. It's nearly too good to be true. Be strong and courageous because God is with you until the end of the age.

My God, thank you for seeing me, knowing me, and being with me. I am yours. Even when I am afraid, I will trust in you. I will press on in courage and lean on your strength when I am weak. Be near and speak to me.

MEASURES OF MERCY

He saved us, not on the basis of deeds which we did in righteousness, but in accordance with His mercy, by the washing of regeneration and renewing by the Holy Spirit.

TITUS 3:5 NASB

You get to choose how you will grow, what steps you will take, and how you treat people. Your choices matter. Still, it is even more important to recognize that none of your choices add or take away from your salvation. You are saved by mercy alone.

God's presence in your life is founded on the work of Christ. His sacrifice has made a way for you to be with God for all your days and into eternity. Your victories don't make his sacrifice more potent, and your failures cannot diminish it. May you find immense freedom in this truth. May you lay down your striving and rest in the glorious gift of salvation.

Christ, thank you for the power of your sacrifice and for the renewal of your Spirit in my life. Thank you for redemption that doesn't depend on my skills or abilities.

PERFECT LOVE

There is no fear in love; instead, perfect love drives out fear, because fear involves punishment. So the one who fears is not complete in love.

1 John 4:18 csb

God's perfect love drives out fear, liberates you from shame, and sets you free to walk in the light of his presence. There is no fear in love. As God removes fear from your heart, you no longer worry about how you might mess up. Even when you fail, God's love is strong enough to restore you.

If you are afraid of sinning, you're missing an aspect of God's delightful mercy. It's good to be mindful of your actions, but don't let mindfulness become legalism. Experiencing God's perfect love despite your weaknesses is where true freedom is found.

Loving Lord, thank you for your unending love. Free me from the fear of sin and punishment. Fill my heart with your love and the confidence of your affection.

GIFTS OF GRACE

As each has received a gift, use it to serve one another, as good stewards of God's varied grace.

1 PETER 4:10 ESV

Your talents, gifts, and strengths are not only for your own benefit. You were created for community, and each person has an important role to play. You can use your gifts to love and serve the people around you. Resist the pull of society to monetize every passion and instead know when to offer specific gifts and services as a generous offering to others.

How can you use your natural strengths, interests, or talents to serve people in your community? Recognize what you have to give and what you are willing to offer. By God's grace you can implement actionable levels of service. Even if you start small, that small beginning is a beautiful representation of God's kingdom.

Gracious God, thank you for the example of service you showed us through Christ. I don't want to forget the importance of connectedness and community. Show me ways I can use my gifts to serve those around me.

CHEERFUL CHOICES

Let each one give as he purposes in his heart, not grudgingly or of necessity; for God loves a cheerful giver.

2 Corinthians 9:7 NKJV

God loves a cheerful giver. There is freedom found in this requirement. God doesn't want you to give because you have to or because you feel guilty. He wants your generosity to be an overflow of what he's done for you. This means that when your giving feels obligatory, you can expect God to meet you in your weakness.

When you are weak, God is strong. He joyfully empowers you when you ask him to. He won't turn you away, and he won't guilt you into obedience. Instead, he will gently address your frustrations and hesitancies. Let go of the need to give and allow God to show you the joy of opening your hands to others.

Generous One, thank you for your abundant gifts. I want to be more like you in my giving. I will not give grudgingly or because I feel pressured to. Help me cultivate joyful generosity in my life.

SPACE FOR GRACE

Always be humble and gentle. Be patient with each other, making allowance for each other's faults because of your love.

EPHESIANS 4:2 NLT

Having a humble and gentle heart will serve you well. It will also be a great benefit to the people around you. Everyone is human and prone to error, and it is a blessing to overlook offenses. When you leave room for other's faults, there is space for grace. When you love people despite their inability to measure up in certain ways, you demonstrate the love of Jesus.

With patience as a priority, you can walk through your faults and flaws with the people in your life. You can encourage your friends when they fail, and you can confidently share your own mistakes knowing they won't shame you. Vulnerability and humility cultivate intimacy, and intimacy allows us to spur each other toward Jesus.

Faithful One, you are so patient and gentle with me. Why would I refuse to do the same with others? Thank you for empowering me by your Spirit to love well.

OPPORTUNITIES TO BLESS

Take advantage of every opportunity to be a blessing to others, especially to our brothers and sisters in the family of faith!

GALATIANS 6:10 TPT

When you cultivate generosity in your heart and life, you will begin to look for opportunities to bless others instead of just waiting for them to appear. Every chance to bless someone is an opportunity for more joy in your own life.

Scripture says to outdo each other in honor and respect. This communicates that there is no limit to the amount of kindness you can show to the people around you. Has someone been thoughtful or respectful toward you? In response, be even more thoughtful, kind, or respectful to the next person you encounter. Devote yourself to creating joy for others and you will not be left empty handed. There is great satisfaction in blessing others.

Marvelous One, I truly want to be part of a body of believers that tries to outdo each other in offering practical kindness, respect, and honor. Help me see opportunities to bless others.

POWERFUL PRUDENCE

The tongue is a small part of the body, but it makes great boasts. Consider what a great forest is set on fire by a small spark.

JAMES 3:5 NIV

Just one small comment can set off a fiery argument. It shows wisdom when you practice prudence with your words, reining in your tongue when you need to. There is power in the words you speak. Don't treat them as meaningless because they have the ability to either build up or tear down the hearer.

As you engage in conversation today, whether face to face or through technology, be sure to pick your words wisely. You don't have to be perfect, but you do need to practice prudence. Consider the impact of your words before you say, write, or type them. Everything you say has an impact, and you are the only one who can control your words.

Wise Father, help me to think through what I say. I don't want to be foolish, causing harm with thoughtless words. May I be wise and thoughtful, just as you are at all times.

SPIRIT OF TRUTH

"When the Spirit of truth comes, he will guide you into all truth. He will not speak on his own but will tell you what he has heard."

JOHN 16:13 NLT

The Spirit of God is the Spirit of truth. There is no other. The Holy Spirit guides you into the ways of God, the truth of his nature, and the incomparable goodness of his kingdom. He reveals God to you, deepening your understanding beyond what you could grasp on your own.

If you are in Christ, you are no longer waiting for the Spirit of truth to come. The Holy Spirit has already been poured out. He is your helper, comforter, and guide in everything you do. Jesus knew that you would struggle to stay faithful to the truth, so he mercifully gave you the gift of the Spirit. He has equipped you fully to follow him.

Spirit, thank you for continually guiding me into truth. I am not afraid of wandering, for I am following your leadership. May the eyes of my heart be enlightened even more as I seek you.

MORE THAN IDEOLOGY

The kingdom of God is not in words, but in power.

1 Corinthians 4:20 NASB

The power of God is not in what he says he will do, but in what he actually does. This is true in your life as well. If you are able to talk a good game but fail to follow through, then your words are meaningless. However, if you do what you say, then you back up your words with the weight of your actions.

God's kingdom is not an ideology. It's not just a nice idea about something that might happen. It is an actual place with an actual reigning King. You may not yet see it, but you catch glimpses of it on the earth as God releases his mercy and faithfully follows through on his Word. Today, remind yourself of the great power of God's kingdom.

King Jesus, I know that your promises are not empty. You are working in my life and in the world around me. Expand my understanding even more today and reveal how you are working here and now.

MULTIPLIED EFFORTS

The one who provides seed for the sower and bread for food will also provide and multiply your seed and increase the harvest of your righteousness.

2 Corinthians 9:10 CSB

As you follow God and seek to do his will, he multiplies your efforts. He is able to do more with your meagre offerings than you could ever imagine. He takes whatever you give him, and he increases its value. He creates an abundant harvest from a single seed.

At the end of the day, God is the one who makes things grow. He is the one who provides for you, and he is the one who cultivates fruit in your life. Commit your ways to him and trust that he will handle the outcome. Put your life in his hands, and he will show you a plentiful harvest.

Generous Father, thank you for your power that multiplies provision. Thank you that cultivating fruit is not my responsibility. I trust you to take what I give you and create something beautiful. You are wonderful.

PERFECT PORTION

"The Lord is my portion," says my soul,
"therefore I will hope in him."

Lamentations 3:24 ESV

God is your perfect portion. He has more than enough grace for anything you might lack. He has overwhelming mercy for your missteps and abundant peace for your fear. Whatever your needs are today, God is an abundantly generous provider.

Open your hands to receive from the overflow of God's goodness. He longs to give you good gifts. He has what you need in every situation. He is the perfect father, friend, teacher, and king. The Lord is your portion. He is capable of filling the cracks in your life no matter how gaping they seem.

Perfect Lord, you are more than enough for every need I have. I trust that you won't let me down, and you won't disregard me. My heart overflows with gratitude for all that you are. I love you.

HOPEFUL RETURNS

"Return to the stronghold,
you prisoners of hope.
Even today I declare
that I will restore double to you."

ZECHARIAH 9:12 NKJV

God is a master restorer. He not only fixes what was broken, but he multiplies what was lost and returns it to you. He is so very good. He goes above and beyond what is necessary, and he joyfully shares the abundance of his goodness.

Salvation alone is an incredible gift. Even so, God does not stop there. You have been saved unto something even greater. You have been saved so that you might experience the eternal pleasure of God's presence. Not only has he redeemed your soul, but he has blessed you with his comfort, wisdom, peace, and guidance. He provides what you need to survive and to thrive.

Faithful One, I trust you with my heart and my life. I know that you are good, and all my hope is in you.

SENSE OF BELONGING

He gave himself for us so he might pay the price to free us from all evil and to make us pure people who belong only to him—people who are always wanting to do good deeds.

Titus 2:14 NCV

Jesus gave himself for you. That is no small statement. He gave himself for you so that you could be free. He paid the price no one else could pay. He did it so that you could know him without any doubt or barrier between you.

You belong in the kingdom of Christ. There is a place specifically for you. No one can take it away from you, and no one can replace you. You are his, and he loves you more than you can imagine. If you struggle to find your place in this world, know that you need not struggle to find yourself in him. He sees you fully, and he loves you endlessly.

Savior, I cannot begin to describe my gratitude for all that you did on the cross. Thank you for saving me. I am yours, and I find myself at home in you.

NOVEMBER

He who started a good work in you will carry it on to completion until the day of Christ Jesus.

PHILIPPIANS 1:6 CSB

EVERY GENERATION

Yahweh is always good and ready to receive you. He's so loving that it will amaze you—so kind that it will astound you! And he is famous for his faithfulness toward all. Everyone knows our God can be trusted, for he keeps his promises to every generation!

Psalm 100:5 TPT

The Lord is good and ready to receive you today. His faithfulness is not reserved for an elite few. He is known for his faithfulness toward all. He is trustworthy and true throughout the ages and to every generation.

Let this be a jumping off point for your own personal experience with God today. He is closer than you realize and more powerful than you know. You don't have to hesitate because his arms are always wide open. Run into the arms of your Lord and be loved to life in his presence.

Wonderful Lord, you are faithful to every promise and every generation. Thank you for the power of your love that spans every distance. Refresh me in your kindness and the truth of your love.

UNSHAKEABLE

Since we are receiving a kingdom that cannot be shaken, let us be thankful, and so worship God acceptably with reverence and awe.

Hebrews 12:28 NIV

Throughout life you will experience many different types of loss. You'll grow, change, and experience heart ache. You'll travel down a different path than you expected, or you'll suffer in a way you didn't see coming. Life is painful for everyone in different ways. The only thing that remains perfectly steady is God's kingdom.

Having been adopted into God's family, you are part of the unshakeable kingdom. When everything around or within you feels chaotic, lean on the one thing that never changes. God is always the same, and his kingdom is secure. Rest in his presence and be comforted by his steadiness.

Worthy God, you are unbreakable and unshakeable. Your power is not threatened by any person or nation. Thank you for the sense of belonging I find in you.

PATIENT ENDURANCE

Do not throw away this confident trust in the Lord. Remember the great reward it brings you! Patient endurance is what you need now, so that you will continue to do God's will. Then you will receive all that he has promised.

HEBREWS 10:35-36 NLT

When hard times linger longer than expected, it can be tempting to give up. It's normal to question your faith and doubt God's goodness. God is not surprised by your weariness. He is not shocked even when your faith is at its weakest. When you feel as if you can't go on, he is there to steady your steps.

Lay your doubts at the feet of Jesus. Remember God's faithfulness and don't give up your confident trust in him! The moment you feel like quitting is exactly when you need to press in the most. Turn toward him and dare to boldly give him your worries and fears. Put your faith in the one who promises to carry you through every valley.

Faithful One, I need the grace of your presence to help me. Help me to endure through seasons of pain. Give me patience and unwavering hope as I lean on you.

EYES THAT SEE

Our struggle is not against flesh and blood, but against the rulers, against the powers, against the world forces of this darkness, against the spiritual forces of wickedness in the heavenly places.

EPHESIANS 6:12 NASB

When you struggle with those around you, it is not a fight against them personally. There are forces at work that you cannot see. Don't lose sight of this and allow your heart to grow cold toward others. Pursuing unity and loving sacrificially is easier when you look beyond the obvious circumstances.

Through the Spirit you gain God's perspective. He offers you eyes to see and ears to hear. He sees past the actions of people and into their hearts. Join with him and look through his lens. As you put on love and heed the wisdom of God, your eyes will be opened to the humanity of those you struggle with.

Perfect One, I don't want to hate those who are different than me, and I don't want to foolishly fight against them when it is not a worthwhile fight. Help me to see from your perspective.

ABUNDANCE

God is able to make every grace overflow to you, so that in every way, always having everything you need, you may excel in every good work.

2 Corinthians 9:8 CSB

God is not in the business of giving you the bare minimum needed for survival. He does not offer you his leftovers or the crumbs that have fallen from his table. He invites you to feast with him. Through Christ, he has made room for you at his banquet table. He gives you what you need and blesses you further so you can share with others.

God wants his grace to overflow in your life. He wants you to know that he longs to give you everything you need to follow him. When you feel as though you are lacking, ask him to remind you of his abundant faithfulness. He will never withhold his grace from you.

Generous God, thank you for the abundance of your gifts in my life. I am so very grateful for your faithfulness to me. Help me to generously share all you've given me.

MIGHTY POWER

The message of the cross is foolishness to those who are perishing, but to us who are being saved it is the power of God.

1 Corinthians 1:18 NKJV

The message of the cross seems foolish to those who don't walk in the ways of Christ. The principles of the kingdom are unfathomable to those who haven't experienced the love of the Lord. It doesn't make sense that Jesus would experience great suffering on behalf of flawed humanity.

The audacious truth of the gospel is what makes it so powerful. The power of God displayed through Jesus is life-changing and miraculous. Don't worry about what other people think of your faith. People might ridicule your decisions, but you can stay steady and keep trusting in the saving power of Christ's love.

Lord Jesus, keep from ever viewing your message as foolishness. Protect me from the bitterness and cynicism that comes from following my own ways. Keep my heart soft, and may I embrace your truth for all my days.

BE MINDFUL

Everything created by God is good, and nothing is to be rejected if it is received with thanksgiving.

1 Timothy 4:4 ESV

It's dangerous to turn your external actions into issues of morality or salvation. It's comfortable to depend on behaviors or habits because they can be easily defined. It's normal to want to draw spiritual conclusions from a list of rules or standards to follow. However, this is exactly the trap Jesus warned the Pharisees of.

The gospel was revolutionary because it focuses on the heart rather behavior. Jesus laid his down so you wouldn't have to be enslaved to a list of rules. Be mindful of the things in your life that make you feel like a successful Christian. Good habits can be useful, but they cannot replace a humble and contrite heart. Your personal relationship with Jesus is more important than your ability to do the right thing.

Lord, thank you for the freedom I have in you to choose what I consume and what I don't. I'm grateful for this, and I don't want to fall in the trap of moralizing anyone's eating habits.

REFINING FIRES

In every way we show we are servants of God: in accepting many hard things, in troubles, in difficulties, and in great problems.

2 CORINTHIANS 6:4 NCV

Difficult times can reveal your character in ways that peaceful times cannot. A storm quickly reveals where your trust lies. When you learn to accept hard things without running away from them, you show that you have strength and perseverance.

Trials create an opportunity to press in with patient endurance. Patient endurance builds your character. The more you lean on God through difficult seasons, the stronger your faith becomes. You don't have to do this out of your own strength. Instead, the Holy Spirit is the one who gives you grace to rely on the Lord. He reminds you of truth, and he comforts you when you are weary.

Holy Spirit, give the grace to depend on God through trials. May difficulties only cause me to become more like you. Give me endurance to remain steady through troubles of every kind.

EASY TO DISCOVER

He has done this so that every person would long for God, feel their way to him, and find him—for he is the God who is easy to discover!

ACTS 17:27 TPT

God is not far from you. He is so very easy to discover. He has put a longing in your heart to discover him, and he won't keep you searching. You were created with a need for connection with your Maker. Finding your identity in him is as natural as breathing.

Consider how you most easily connect to God. Think about how you naturally see him move in the world. Is it in the outdoors, through music, or through reading his Word? Spend time doing whatever causes you to be filled with awe toward God. Turn your eyes toward him with confidence that you will find what you are looking for.

Wonderful One, thank you for making yourself so easy to find. You don't hide in an obscure place that I may or may not stumble upon. You are close to me even now. Open my eyes to your presence.

SEASONED WITH GRACE

Let your conversation be always full of grace, seasoned with salt, so that you may know how to answer everyone.

COLOSSIANS 4:6 NIV

When you drench your conversations in grace, you make room for the truth and clarity of God's Word. May the words you say be founded in truth and love no matter who you are talking to. Be mindful of what you say and consciously use your words to point others to Jesus.

When you speak with grace, you allow others to be vulnerable and honest. You can hold firmly to the truth and still be defined by gentleness and mercy. This way of communicating allows God's character to shine through. He never speaks down to you or holds his standards over your head in a condescending way. May your words toward others do the same.

Gracious God, help me to keep every conversation seasoned with grace. May my words be honoring to you. May everything I say make space for your mercy and grace to move in the lives of others.

REFRESHING PERSPECTIVES

Let my teaching fall on you like rain;
let my speech settle like dew.
Let my words fall like rain on tender grass,
like gentle showers on young plants.

DEUTERONOMY 32:2 NLT

God's teachings do not come down hard and fast like an anvil falling from the sky. They are more like gentle rain and dew that gathers. His words are refreshing and life-giving. He does not find satisfaction in one upping you, and he doesn't prove his point with harshness or pride.

God communicates with you with so much grace and mercy. When he speaks, his words are delightful and lovely. His kindness is what stirs you to follow him. Let your heart rest in the ease of his presence. Breathe in the sweetness of his character and open your heart to him. If you allow him to, he will lead you with gentleness and bring fresh life to the broken parts of your heart.

Kind Father, thank you for your incredible kindness. Thank you for speaking to me so patiently and mercifully. Your presence is so refreshing and life-giving. Help me find rest and peace in your arms.

SHARPENED BY WISDOM

If the axe is dull and he does not sharpen its edge,
Then he must exert more strength.
Wisdom has the advantage of giving success.

ECCLESIASTES 10:10 NASB

There's no need to rely on your own intellect when you have access to the abundant wisdom of God. He has promised to give you wisdom without restraint when you ask for it. Refusing to pursue wisdom is like insisting on chopping wood with a dull axe when a razor sharp one is sitting next to you.

God offers you his wisdom as a gift. His hands are open, and he is always ready to share. Find joy in fully utilizing the tools he's given you. Steer clear of pridefully proving yourself. It doesn't make sense to depend on your own abilities when God offers you so much more. However far you can go on your own, God can take you even farther.

Lord, I know that your wisdom is full of grace, truth, and power. I don't want to rely on my own limited understanding today. I welcome your wisdom, strategies, and the power of your perspective in every area of my life.

EVERY SINGLE DAY

Encourage each other daily, while it is still called today, so that none of you is hardened by sin's deception.

HEBREWS 3:13 CSB

Every day is an opportunity to encourage people in your life. As you lean on each other, you can support and inspire one another to remain strong in God's love and open to his wisdom and correction. You can encourage each other and remind each other of the truth.

You need the support of other believers. You were created for fellowship and communion. While everyone experiences seasons of loneliness, it isn't the ideal situation. Each person is a beautiful representation of who God is, and together we provide a clearer picture of the totality of his character. You need the gifts, personalities, and understanding of other believers especially when they are different from yours.

Present One, thank you for the people in my life who are living examples of your love and truth. I do not take them for granted. As I go about my day, show me ways I can offer encouragement to those around me.

SPRINGS OF LIFE

"Behold, I am doing a new thing;
now it springs forth, do you not perceive it?
I will make a way in the wilderness
and rivers in the desert."

ISAIAH 43:19 ESV

God is always moving. He is never stagnant or uncaring. He is constantly intervening on behalf of his people. If you don't see evidence of his mercy, ask the Holy Spirit to open your eyes. God never changes which means that your perspective needs to shift.

Partner with God and he will give you eyes to see. Perhaps your senses have been dulled by the mundane details of life. Maybe you've let disappointment cloud your perception of God's goodness. Today is a fresh opportunity to be joyfully surprised by his faithfulness. Ask him to renew your perspective, and he will do it.

Redeemer, I'm so grateful that there is always newness in you. No matter how many endings I face in this life, there are always new beginnings to be found. Thank you.

LET HIM DO IT

Humble yourselves in the sight of the Lord,
and He will lift you up.

JAMES 4:10 NKJV

Don't run away when you feel the pain of your mistakes. Don't shy away from the regret of a bad decision. Take your frustrations to the Lord and allow yourself to feel disappointed. Don't brush away your emotions. Rather, let the Lord lead you through them.

Bringing your guilt, worry, and disappointment to God is the most productive way of dealing with your emotions. Humble yourself before him and invite him into the depths of your heart. Instead of trying to sort through everything alone, trust him to give you direction. Lay it all down at the feet of the Lord and he will lift you up.

Lord, thank you for the power of your mercy that heals, restores, and redeems. I won't try to escape sorrow when it settles in, and I won't try to run away from the pain of regret. Help me and lift me up in my weakness.

MAKE A CHANGE

"Change your hearts and lives because the kingdom of heaven is near."

MATTHEW 3:2 NCV

John the Baptist prepared people's hearts for the ministry of Jesus. He paved the way for Jesus to come forward and change the lives of everyone he met. The invitation to change your heart and life remains as poignant today. You are still called to be aware of the coming kingdom.

Don't put off for another day the changes you want to make in your life. Every small step is meaningful. Don't look at the end goal and be intimidated by the distances between now and then. Do what you can today and know that it is enough. Every glance toward the Lord counts.

Jesus Christ, help me to take the steps I need to today. Show me how to prepare for the coming kingdom. Help me turn toward you in greater measure.

EVERY DETAIL

"Don't worry. For your Father cares deeply about even the smallest detail of your life."

MATTHEW 10:30 TPT

God doesn't overlook any part of your life. He cares deeply about even the smallest details. Let that sink in. If you have any worries today, God can be trusted to take care of them whether they are big or small. No matter what the details are, God is capable of taking care of whatever you put in his hands.

God doesn't miss anything. He doesn't forget the things that slip your mind. You don't have to worry. He covers the cracks in your life with his overpowering mercy. He is capable of compensating for your faults and weaknesses. Trust him with the details. You may not know how things will work out, but he does. He is attentive, kind, and able to care for you.

Faithful Father, I trust you to take care of me in both big and little ways. I believe that you are trustworthy and true. Thank you.

CULTIVATING LOVE

Whoever would foster love covers over an offense,
but whoever repeats the matter separates close friends.

PROVERBS 17:9 NIV

Love does not look for reasons to hold grudges. It doesn't dwell on others' mistakes. Love chooses to overlook the mistakes of others rather than holding on to them in a search for vindication. Love doesn't look for validation, but it puts the needs of others first.

Imagine what your relationships could look like if this principle were enacted. How many times have you held onto annoyances or offense? How many times have you let the actions of others dictate how you treat them or what you think of them? True love which covers offenses seems too good to be true. This is why you need to rely on God's strength. He loves perfectly and he is the only one who can equip you to do it.

God, there isn't anyone who overlooks more faults than you do. Fill my heart with your love and help me to choose to let go of the minor things that don't matter. Thank you.

HIDE IN HIM

You are my hiding place;
you protect me from trouble.
You surround me with songs of victory.

PSALM 32:7 NLT

If you feel the urge to hide at all, hide yourself in the canopy of God's presence. If you want to quit and run away, run into his arms and find refuge there. He will protect you from trouble, and he will surround you with the songs of his victory. His presence is full of perfect peace, stable wisdom, and uplifting hope. He calms anxious hearts and watches over the vulnerable.

Run into the shelter of God's love when your feet are ready to race from your circumstances. Even if you physically don't move a muscle, your heart and soul can find rest in the presence of his peace. He is near. Bring him every care, worry, and question you have. It's okay to run and hide if you need to. Run to God, for he is a safe place of shelter.

Victorious One, you are my hiding place. I come to you whenever my heart needs a place to take shelter. Thank you for faithfully protecting me in your love. You are my strong foundation, and I won't run from you.

TASTE AND SEE

Taste and see that the Lord is good;
How blessed is the man who takes refuge in Him!

Psalm 34:8 NASB

The Lord is good. This is a truth that always remains. If it has been a while since you tasted his goodness, come and feast in his presence. If you have not recognized the loving-kindness of God in your own life, consider this your invitation.

Blessed are you when you run to hide in the shelter of God's love. He is a safe place at all times. You will taste the goodness of the Lord. You will see how wonderful he is toward you. Believe that God has good things in store for you. Go to him with the expectation that he will care for you. As long as you draw breath into your lungs, the goodness of God is near.

Good Father, you are exceedingly good to all who look to you for help. I won't stop coming to you over and over again with the hunger of my heart. I want to taste and see your goodness in fresh and new ways today.

CHOOSING EMPATHY

Rejoice with those who rejoice; weep with those who weep.

ROMANS 12:15 CSB

Loving others often means meeting them where they are. It takes intentionality to set aside your own emotions and tend to the emotions of others. Grieve with those who are grieving. Trying to convince someone to feel different doesn't help. Instead, love them with the same gentle and steady love that you get from God.

Sometimes it's actually easier to offer solace to grief than to rejoice when others succeed. Both are equally important. If someone receives something you want, celebrate with them! If someone is happy, hopeful, and joyous, join them! It takes humility to set aside your own disappointments, but it is always worth it.

Merciful Father, thank you for the power of your love that rejoices with those who celebrate and weeps with those who weep. I have known the power of empathy in my own life, and I choose to grow in it in relation to those around me.

GIVE CREDIT

The horse is made ready for the day of battle,
but the victory belongs to the LORD.

PROVERBS 21:31 ESV

Victory belongs to the Lord. As you partner with him, you can trust that he will reign no matter what happens. You can prepare for a battle as much as possible, but God is the one who dictates the outcome. He is the one who deserves the true credit.

God is the source of every good thing in your life. It can be tempting to boast about your abilities, habits, character traits, and successes. The truth is that every tool you've relied on has come from God. Don't pridefully attribute your victories to your own skills. Instead, humbly acknowledge your Maker. Praise him for all he's done and rely on him for every battle to come.

God, you are the victorious one who reigns over all. In you, I find peace, hope, and strength. You are worthy of all my praise and worship.

LIVING FOR GOODNESS

Seek good and not evil,
That you may live;
So the LORD God of hosts will be with you,
As you have spoken.

AMOS 5:14 NKJV

Deliberately seek after God's goodness and you will experience it. He does not withhold anything from his children. He is not stingy, and he is not selfish. If you are determined to see his goodness while you are living, you will. This is because once you've trained your eyes to see it, you'll realize that it is everywhere.

God's goodness isn't intangible. It's not simply an idea you chase. His goodness is found in the glory of creation, the beauty of his Word, and the comfort and peace of his presence. Don't limit yourself to obvious displays of his power. Instead, train yourself to see every little hidden treasure. His fingerprints are everywhere.

Mighty God, open my eyes to see your goodness. Help me to consistently choose good over evil. Thank you for the wonderful gifts you've given me in your presence.

CANNOT BE CONTAINED

"I am a God who is near," says the LORD.
"I am also a God who is far away.
No one can hide where I cannot see him," says the LORD.
"I fill all of heaven and earth," says the LORD.

JEREMIAH 23:23-24 NCV

The Lord God cannot be contained, and he cannot be pinned down. He is both near and far. He is vast and palpable. His presence is everywhere, for he is Spirit. He fills all of heaven and earth. His goodness is beyond your understanding, and his greatness is more than you can comprehend.

With this in mind, allow you expectations of God to expand. He is more powerful, kind, and good than you think. You can accurately assume that however you see God, he is more. He exists far outside the scope of your humanity. He is not bound by the things that bind you. He is so much greater!

Inescapable One, you cannot be pinned down. I don't want to dumb you down to my level. I want to transform in the grandiosity of who you are. May the expectations of my faith grow even as my imagination stretches to know you more.

STILL REJOICING

We may suffer, yet in every season we are always found rejoicing. We may be poor, yet we bestow great riches on many. We seem to have nothing, yet in reality we possess all things.

2 Corinthians 6:10 TPT

When you go through hard seasons where the suffering is long and the pain is deep, may you still be found rejoicing in the goodness of your God. No matter how little you may have to your name, there is still much that you can offer others. Even when it seems as if you have nothing the world values, you have riches in the kingdom of Christ.

What greater reason to rejoice is there than knowing that you are loved by the Lord? No matter what season you are in, look for the light that still shines through. God is as close as he ever was. There are pockets of peace and moments of miraculous mercy. Even now, you are filled with the abundance of Christ.

Lord, may I still be found rejoicing even in suffering. You are my goodness, my present peace, and my reason to celebrate in every season. I love you.

FULL OF COMPASSION

Praise be to the God and Father of our Lord Jesus Christ, the Father of compassion and the God of all comfort.

2 Corinthians 1:3 niv

God is the Father of compassion. He is the God of all comfort. When you are heartbroken, he is near. He knows you just as you are; he sees your weaknesses, and he reads the pain of your heart. Even when you can't figure out our own distress, you are not a mystery to him.

There is no need to hide how you're really feeling from the Lord. He already knows the depths of your emotions. You don't have to dress yourself up or pretend that you are fine when you are not. He does not want your best self; he just wants you. Allow him to minister to the parts of you that so desperately need his compassion and comfort. In him, your soul can find rest, refreshment, and relief.

Compassionate Father, I don't know why I try to hide my pain from you. You already know it well. I receive your comfort and compassion today. Lift the weight of my burdens with the comfort of your presence.

GREAT EXPECTATION

It is by his great mercy that we have been born again. Now we live with great expectation, and we have a priceless inheritance—an inheritance that is kept in heaven for you, pure and undefiled, beyond the reach of change and decay.

1 PETER 1:3-4 NLT

You experience renewal and transformation in the presence of God. He breathes life into your soul, and you are born again. Every good thing comes from the Father. Every perfect gift is from his hand. Every act of pure love reflects his own. May you look for the fingerprints of his mercy in the world around you, for he is alive and moving in your midst.

You can have great expectations, not only for eternal life in God's kingdom, but also for the life you live now. There is hope and comfort in his presence. He is the embodiment of joy, power, and faithfulness. Though you only get glimpses of his glory now, one day you will see it fully.

Glorious God, there is no one greater than you. All of my hopes are set on you. I trust that your love will never fail. Even when I falter, you are faithful. I worship you.

ALWAYS A WAY

No temptation has overtaken you except something common to mankind; and God is faithful, so He will not allow you to be tempted beyond what you are able, but with the temptation will provide the way of escape also, so that you will be able to endure it.

1 Corinthians 10:13 NASB

Jesus spent forty days in the wilderness being tempted in every way. He withstood each and every trial he faced. He remained strong in faith and refused to trade his relationship with the Father for something that would never satisfy. You can follow his example with confidence because he promises to help you.

Even if you have fallen a thousand times, you can still choose a different way today. Temptations are common, but God is faithful. He has given you everything you need to remain strong no matter what comes your way.

Righteous One, in your victory, I find victory. I trust you to help me when I am tempted to choose another way than your love. Thank you for your help and redemption.

JUST A SHADOW

"Who am I, and who are my people, that we should be able to give as generously as this? For everything comes from you, and we have given you only what comes from your own hand. For we are aliens and temporary residents in your presence as were all our ancestors. Our days on earth are like a shadow, without hope."

1 Chronicles 29:14-15 CSB

Your life is only a shadow in the grand scheme of things. Your time on earth is incredibly short compared to the time you will spend in eternity. One person is barely a blip on the timeline, but God ascribes incredible value to your existence.

God is mindful of you. He sees you clearly among billions of other people. He knows the details of your days, and she sees the overall trajectory of your life. He holds you firmly in his hands and consistently gives you what you need.

Almighty God, thank you for all that you have given me. I offer it right back to you in gratitude. Thank you for loving me. I can't help but love you, for you are incredibly good to me.

ABIDE IN TRUTH

His anointing teaches you about everything, and is true, and is no lie—just as it has taught you, abide in him.

1 John 2:27 ESV

The anointing is not some mysterious thing that some get and some don't. God's anointing is the presence of the Holy Spirit. The anointing of the Spirit brings life, illumination, the fruit of Christ's kingdom, power, and wisdom. He teaches you the truth, and he reveals the ways of God to your heart.

Abide in the Holy Spirit and make him your home. Commune with him in the secret place of your soul. Open yourself to his leadership and trust he won't let you go astray. He will keep you steady and point you toward Christ in all things. He will teach you wisdom and correct you with gentleness. The Spirit is a wonderful gift who is always near.

Holy Spirit, you are the anointing of God who teaches me to walk in the wisdom and ways of Christ. I submit to your leadership, and I partner with your purposes. Be at home in me, even as I find myself at home in you.

DECEMBER

I meditate on you during the night watches
because you are my helper.

Psalm 63:6-7 CSB

STAY THE COURSE

Do not turn aside; for then you would go after empty things which cannot profit or deliver, for they are nothing.

1 SAMUEL 12:21 NKJV

Following the path God has for you is your best option. He doesn't ask you to do certain things for no reason. Each of his standards and instructions have a purpose. He knows what is best for you, and he knows how to lead you.

Wandering away from God's path for your life might seem like an act of personal defiance or independence, but it's not actually in your best interest. Even when you don't see the whole picture clearly, God knows exactly what is right for your life. You can trust his leadership because he has your well-being in mind.

Lord, no matter where I go or what I do, you are at the center of it all. Where I have cut corners or lost sight of what is important, open my eyes. Help me remain grounded in your love.

SENT TO SAVE

"God did not send his Son into the world to judge the world guilty, but to save the world through him."

John 3:17 NCV

When you share the message of Christ's life, death, and resurrection, the focus should be on salvation not judgment. For God did not send his Son to point out flaws and create shame. He sent him to save the world.

It can be tempting to hyperfocus on the things other people do incorrectly. Remember the incredible grace that has been freely given to you. Seek to empower others with mercy and grace in the same way God empowers you. He doesn't expect you to do everything correctly all the time. You display his love when you treat others in the same way.

Savior, thank you for the power of your love that sets the captive free and gives sight to the blind. You are exceedingly good. May my life point others toward your love and salvation.

CONFIDENCE IN CRISIS

God is your confidence in times of crisis,
keeping your heart at rest in every situation.

PROVERBS 3:26 TPT

There isn't a single moment in your life when the peace of God is unavailable to you. No matter how stressful your circumstances are, your heart can be at rest. You don't have to worry about worst case scenarios or potential pitfalls. God your confidence in times of crisis.

How can you hold onto God even in times of crisis? As you cultivate deep friendship with him and rely on his Spirit, you build a bridge of trust that cannot be broken. Don't neglect the power of the relationship you have with the Lord. He is near, and he is faithful through every trial and triumph.

Faithful God, you give me rest, even in raging storms. You are my safe place, and I can never lose you. Thank you for being my confidence in every season and stage. I trust you.

COMPLETELY FAMILIAR

You discern my going out and my lying down;
you are familiar with all my ways.
Before a word is on my tongue,
you, LORD, know it completely.

PSALM 139:3-4 NIV

The God who created you knows you better than anyone else. You are not a mystery to him. He loves you through and through. He hems you in behind and before, keeping watch over you. There is so much goodness, peace, and strength in choosing to follow his ways. He will not lead you astray.

When you are confident in God's awareness of you, each step you take will be steady and sure. When you fully believe that he is constantly taking care of you, your worries will begin to fade away. God sees you, knows you, and loves you perfectly.

Lord, I am humbled to know that you know me and love me thoroughly. Why would I look for satisfaction apart from you? Your love is the fuel to my heart, my life, and my hope. I love you.

DIFFERENT EXPRESSIONS

God works in different ways, but it is the same God who does the work in all of us.

1 Corinthians 12:6 NLT

Your life isn't supposed to look exactly like the people around you. The details of your days will be different, and your path will have different stops and detours. Don't compare your perceived successes and failures with others. Remember that God is perfectly orchestrating each person's life.

There is peace in staying in your own lane with your eyes turned heavenward. As you depend on God for direction, you can trust that he will lead you according to this will. He will work in and through your life exactly as he pleases. You don't need to fret when you're unsure how the pieces of your life will fit together. God knows, and you can trust him.

God, thank you for the freedom I find in you. I follow the path you have laid out for me, even if I don't see the whole picture. I trust you.

MIGHTY FAITH

Though you have not seen Him, you love Him, and though you do not see Him now, but believe in Him, you greatly rejoice with joy inexpressible and full of glory.

1 Peter 1:8 NASB

God is delighted by your faith. He sees every step you take toward him whether it is big or small. He acknowledges that you have devoted your life to Jesus even though you've never seen him. He knows that you love him even though your eyes haven't gazed upon his physical face.

Don't discredit your faith just because you might think it's small. Your desire to follow God and do the right thing shows great faith. Your declaration that God is real and Jesus rose from the dead is powerful. Be encouraged and move forward with intention. Walk along the path God has for you knowing that he is proud of you because you are his child.

Lord, thank you for the faith you've given me. Thank you for drawing me to your heart and transforming my life. Fill me with your love and strengthen me to continue doing your will.

HE IS COMING

"Sing and rejoice, O daughter of Zion! For behold, I am coming and I will dwell in your midst," says the LORD. "Many nations shall be joined to the LORD in that day, and they shall become My people. And I will dwell in your midst. Then you will know that the LORD of hosts has sent Me to you."

ZECHARIAH 2:10-11 NKJV

You are still waiting to experience the fullness of God's kingdom. He promises that he will wipe every tear from your eyes, and the pain of death will be but a memory. You will be united with his sons and daughters from every tribe, nation, and language. Until that day, you wait with hope.

As you wait, you have the power of Christ's resurrection as your own triumph. You have been brought close to God in his mercy, and every accusation against you is silenced in the power of his love. You have been purified, redeemed, and liberated. Don't lose sight of the hope of your calling, for God is with you now in Spirit until you dwell with him in the fullness of his promise.

King Jesus, I am so grateful for glimpses of your glorious kingdom in this world and in my life. I wait with hope for the day that you will reign fully and completely and silence every other competing voice.

BELIEVE IT

"I tell you, whatever you ask in prayer, believe that you have received it, and it will be yours."

MARK 11:24 ESV

You are welcomed into God's presence with open arms whenever you approach him. Don't hesitate to pour out your heart to him. Pray and believe that God hears you. The more time you spend with him in prayer, the more confident you will become of his character.

Your faith will be strengthened as you cultivate the habit of prayer. As you pray, do it boldly and without apology. Your God is a good Father, and he delights in you. He hears your prayers when they are well thought out and when they are messy. He loves to partner with you through prayer.

Faithful Lord, I want my faith to grow in the power of your love. As I stretch myself to ask for what I need and long for, I trust you to provide it. Thank you.

OVERFLOWING

"Blessed are those who hunger and thirst for righteousness, for they will be filled."

MATTHEW 5:6 CSB

When you hunger and thirst for righteousness, you will be satisfied. In other words, when you long for the goodness of God, you will find it. When you search for his presence, you won't come up wanting.

There are certain elements in God's kingdom that he shares without restraint. You can be confident that God will give you exactly what you ask for when it aligns with Scripture. There is no limit to the amount of godly character you can have. If you ask him for righteousness, he will give it to you.

Righteous One, though I lacked in righteousness on my own, you gave me your own. Thank you for satisfying my hunger and thirst with the abundance of your goodness and mercy.

HAPPY TO HOST

The believers met together in the Temple every day. They ate together in their homes, happy to share their food with joyful hearts.

Acts 2:46 NCV

There is joy found in sharing what you have. Give generously and with joy when the opportunity arises. It doesn't matter if you have a lot to offer. The point is to hold your material possessions with an open grasp. If God has given you good gifts, don't keep them to yourself.

As you share with others your faith will be strengthened. You will have the satisfaction of creating joy in someone else's life, and you will have the opportunity to trust God for more provision. He is the one who gives you what you need, and you can rely on him to be faithful when you pour your life out for others.

Father, thank you for the many good gifts you've given me. Help me share what I have with generosity and joy. I trust you to provide for me.

MINISTRY OF RECONCILIATION

God has made all things new, and reconciled us to himself, and given us the ministry of reconciling others to God.

2 Corinthians 5:18 TPT

You have been made new in Christ. Your sin stood in the way, but He made a way for you to be close to the Father. You have been restored to friendship with God which is what you were created for. Now that you have a secure relationship with God, you can help draw other people back to him.

You can partner with God in the ministry of reconciliation. You can share Christ's love and sacrifice with those who need it most. The way you speak to and treat others gives them a glimpse of who God is. May your words and actions stir up affection for the Lord.

Redeemer, thank you for making all things new including me. You are better than the best of friends. Your motives are pure and your heart kind. I will partner with your purposes and share your goodness with others.

ALWAYS NEAR

I keep my eyes always on the LORD.
With him at my right hand, I will not be shaken.
Therefore my heart is glad and my tongue rejoices;
my body also will rest secure.

PSALM 16:8-9 NIV

Every day is a fresh chance to fix your eyes on the Lord. He is always near, and his ears are always attuned to your voice. No matter what you walk into today, go with the confidence that God is at your right hand.

No matter what typically causes you anxiety, God is walking alongside you. When worry rises within you, remember his nearness. Remind yourself of the faithfulness of his help and the love he has for you. Look to him for guidance, and he will lead you forward with steadiness.

Lord, thank you for reminding me of my worth, and that it is always rooted in you. I won't be led by fear or anxiety. You are my confidence today and always.

IN SPIRIT AND TRUTH

"The time is coming—indeed it's here now—when true worshipers will worship the Father in spirit and in truth. The Father is looking for those who will worship him that way."

JOHN 4:23 NLT

God doesn't need disingenuous worship. He doesn't want you to praise him because you feel obligated or think it's the right thing to do. If he wanted mindless worship, he could create that for himself. He wants a wholehearted relationship with you because you are his child.

Let your worship of God be honest and real. Bring him the reality of your heart and don't hold anything back. Allow your spirit to commune with his. In his presence, he will transform your heart. As your eyes are turned toward him, he will bless you with his nearness.

Jesus, I worship you in spirit and truth. I know you see my heart, and I don't have to explain myself to you. Thank you for honoring my sincere worship.

SONS AND DAUGHTERS

"I will be a father to you,
And you shall be sons and daughters to Me,"
Says the LORD Almighty.

2 CORINTHIANS 6:18 NASB

In Christ, you have been adopted into the family of God. You are his child, and he delights in you. He longs to take care of you. He knows you better than you know yourself, and he welcomes you into his kingdom with open arms.

No matter what your earthly family looks like, you can lean on the steadiness of God. He is a perfect father. He is patient, kind, attentive, and strong. It is his joy to support and encourage you. He doesn't take care of you because he has to but because he loves you more than anything.

Father, thank you for being the perfect parent. I trust you to receive me with love every time I turn to you. Thank you for being kind even in your correction. I love you.

CALL ON HIM

He himself has suffered when he was tempted, he is able to help those who are tempted.

Hebrews 2:18 CSB

Jesus understands whatever complicated feelings you experience. He knows exactly how it feels to be tempted. Your struggles are not beyond his ability to help you. He can relate to your emotions, and he can strengthen you as you process through them.

Lean on Jesus who is your advocate and friend. When you experience temptation, bring him the totality of your reaction to it. He is the only one who knows exactly what you need. He has what it takes to both comfort you and empower you to move forward. Don't let shame keep you from calling on the name of Jesus when you need him most.

Lord Jesus, thank you for already walking the path of testing and temptation. Thank you for being a relatable advocate. I trust that your help is sufficient. Give me grace as I walk through hard times. You are the one I lean on more than any other.

PRECIOUS PROMISES

He has granted to us his precious and very great promises, so that through them you may become partakers of the divine nature, having escaped from the corruption that is in the world because of sinful desire.

2 Peter 1:4 ESV

Through the promise of Christ, you are able to partner with his divine nature to experience triumph over sin. His mercy covers you completely, and you are liberated in his love. You are no longer bound by fear, shame, sin, or death. There is nothing holding you back from eternal life.

Though you may suffer in this life, one day you will be free from pain. Though you may experience the chaos of corruption in this world, God remains your source of peace. There is no problem he won't fix, and there's no mountain that can't be moved in his power. Today align your heart and choices with the love of Christ that conquers fear.

Jesus Christ, I believe that you are the way, the truth, and the life. I am yours, and I cling to your promises like they are my daily nourishment. May I become even more alive, free, and hopeful in your love today.

DEDICATED TO GOD

"For this child I prayed, and the LORD has granted me my petition which I asked of Him. Therefore I also have lent him to the LORD; as long as he lives he shall be lent to the LORD."

1 SAMUEL 1:27-28 NKJV

When the Lord answers your prayers, what is your response to him? Instead of simply moving on, quickly forgetting both the longing and the poignant provision of God, remember that each answer to prayer is a gift from God.

When prayers are answered, take the time to revel at God's faithfulness. Soak in the satisfaction that comes from experiencing God's tangible provision. Thank him wholeheartedly and fully embrace the gift he's given you. As you deliberately praise him for what he's done, your faith will be strengthened.

Gracious God, thank you for the good and perfect gifts of your love in my life. Thank you for answering the longings of my heart with your provision.

EVEN MORE STRENGTH

He gives strength to those who are tired
and more power to those who are weak.

Isaiah 40:29 NCV

When you are tired, God gives you strength. When you are weak, he offers you his power. The Word of God does not say that those who walk in the ways of the Lord will never tire or grow weary. God knows that you will be tired, but he offers you abundant rest when you turn to him.

No matter how tired you are today, God has strength to empower you. He has grace for your weakness. Lean into his presence and ask him for his help. You don't have to power through on your own. Time with him is the only solution for weariness of your body or soul.

Mighty One, thank you for not demanding strength from me. You accept me in my weakness, offering me your own grace. I rest in you, and I receive your power in the place of my weakness. Thank you.

FREE FROM WORRY

The work of righteousness is peace, and the result of righteousness is quietness and confidence forever. My people will live free from worry in secure, quiet resting places.

Isaiah 32:17-18 TPT

The work of righteousness does not sow dissension but peace. The result of righteousness is not chaos and insecurity but quietness and confidence. If you walk in the ways of righteousness, you will be known as a pursuer of peace.

Even if the world around you is chaotic, you can live in a quiet home of peace. You can cultivate a home that is secure in the love of God and live free from the weight of worry. This doesn't mean that you won't experience trials. It means that the security of your inner self cannot be shaken. No matter what your physical circumstances are, Jesus is your source of quiet rest.

Prince of Peace, I want to be known as a pursuer of peace rather than a stirrer of chaos. You are faithful, and I want to live in the security of your faithfulness all my days. May my home reflect your peace.

GENERATIONS OF FAITHFULNESS

"The Lord is my strength and my defense;
he has become my salvation.
He is my God, and I will praise him,
my father's God, and I will exalt him."

Exodus 15:2 NIV

God is faithful through all generations. He has been present in the lives of his people from the beginning of time. He has woven his mercy into your life in the same way he showed up for Abraham, Isaac, or Jacob. You are part of his eternal and glorious story.

If you want to be encouraged, ask someone who is older than you to tell their story. Listen intently to how God has shown up for them. Be encouraged by his faithfulness in their life. From the beginning of time to the end of all things, God is worthy of your praise.

Faithful One, there is no one like you in all the universe. You are always my strength and my defense. You are my salvation. I trust you. May my heart grow in confidence as I see you in the stories of others.

BROUGHT NEAR

You have been united with Christ Jesus. Once you were far away from God, but now you have been brought near to him through the blood of Christ.

EPHESIANS 2:13 NLT

The blood of Christ is like a bridge. It is a direct connection to God the Father. You can go boldly into his presence without fear because Christ has done all that was necessary for you to be united in peace with God. No matter how far away you were before you knew Jesus, he has completely bridged the gap.

The nearness of God is a truth you must deliberately cling to. You won't always feel close to him, but the truth matters more than your feelings. When you want to believe you are alone, intentionally remind yourself of what's true. The more you declare it, the stronger your faith becomes. Over time, this truth will be an unshakable part of who you are.

Lord Jesus, thank you for the power of your blood that acts as a bridge to bring me close to the Father. Thank you for doing all that was necessary to restore me to the Father's love. I yield to your love today, knowing it is my source and strength.

LIVING HOPE

Blessed be the God and Father of our Lord Jesus Christ, who according to His great mercy has caused us to be born again to a living hope through the resurrection of Jesus Christ from the dead.

1 PETER 1:3 NASB

Jesus Christ is your living hope. Your hope isn't anchored to a far-off dream that never happens or an impossible ideology that is never embodied. Your hope is securely anchored to the person of Jesus Christ. He is alive and well, and he is seated at the right hand of the Father.

It doesn't matter what the circumstances of your life are. It doesn't matter if you move from mountain top to mountain top or make your home in the valley; your hope remains the same. No matter what, you can cling to Jesus. You can rely on him to fulfill every one of God's promises. He is your proven and reliable source of hope.

Faithful Father, thank you for the hope I have in Jesus. Thank you for the safety and peace I find in your promises. Keep me from placing my trust in any lesser loves.

BUILD MUSCLES

Be strengthened by the Lord and by his vast strength.

EPHESIANS 6:10 CSB

You can strengthen your spiritual muscles as practically as you can your physical ones. Spiritual strength training takes discipline and consistency as well as a lot of grace. The road toward spiritual maturity isn't always comfortable but it is always worth it. The stronger you become the steadier you will be through trials and hardships.

Spiritual maturity often starts with humility and teachability. You can't grow if you aren't able to admit your need for growth. As weaknesses show up in your life, you have the opportunity to bring them to the Lord and submit them to his will. In order for him to strengthen you where you are weak you must humbly acknowledge that you need him.

Holy Spirit, thank you for your leadership and wisdom in my life. Help me strengthen my heart, mind, body, and spirit. Increase my faith as I yield to your leadership in all things.

WONDERFUL GOD

To us a child is born, to us a son is given;
and the government shall be upon his shoulder,
and his name shall be called
Wonderful Counselor, Mighty God,
Everlasting Father, Prince of Peace.

Isaiah 9:6 ESV

Jesus is your Wonderful Counselor, Mighty God, Everlasting Father, and Prince of Peace. He is the long-awaited Savior who takes away the sins of the world. He is your peace with God, your everlasting King, and your wise and wonderful Counselor in all things.

As you consider the first coming of Christ on this Christmas Eve, meditate on the glory of God manifested in humanity. Jesus chose to come humbly. Though he dwelt with God from the beginning, he willingly put on flesh and bones so that you could recognize him. He humbled himself so that you would know God. Delight in his kindness and marvel at his humility this Christmas season.

Everlasting God, thank you for the power of your choice to become human in order to save humanity. You are wonderful, and I am in awe of you.

JOYOUS TIDINGS

The angel said to them, "Do not be afraid, for behold, I bring you good tidings of great joy which will be to all people. For there is born to you this day in the city of David a Savior, who is Christ the Lord."

LUKE 2:10-11 NKJV

The birth of Jesus was good news for all. The Savior of the world was born. He humbled himself to the human experience, being born in a stable to poor parents. From the start of his story, he related to the humble and offered hope to the weak.

Jesus is the same today as he was when he walked the earth. He is the same humble and attentive Savior. He came as a baby to set the captives free, heal the sick, and deliver the tormented. From his meagre beginnings to his glorious resurrection, Jesus is your living hope.

Jesus, thank you for coming in the humblest of ways for the hope and salvation of all. Thank you for fulfilling the Father's promise of redemption. You are worthy of the highest praise.

KEEP GOING

We are surrounded by a great cloud of people whose lives tell us what faith means. So let us run the race that is before us and never give up.

HEBREWS 12:1 NCV

When you grow tired, you have only to remember that you are not alone in this race of life. You can be encouraged by those who have gone before you. You can read their stories and be bolstered by their faith. You also have the encouragement of the Spirit and the grace of God to see you through.

Everyone has a race to run. The obstacles might look different, but the finish line is the same. Everyone is on a journey toward the restoration of all things. As you seek to remain faithful for all of your days, remember that God has given you exactly what you need to endure. He faithfully provides you with encouragement and strength whenever you need it.

God, thank you for the power of testimonies. Thank you for the encouragement I can get from hearing the stories of others. Where I am tempted to give up, strengthen me in your mercy.

HE WON'T FORGET

"How could a loving mother forget her nursing child and not deeply love the one she bore? Even if there is a mother who forgets her child, I could never, no never, forget you."

ISAIAH 49:15 TPT

You are seen and fully loved. God's love for you goes beyond the bond of a mother and child. He is more attentive to you than a mother who is nursing her baby. He sees every moment of your day. He knows you better than anyone else, and he is devoted to carrying you through life.

God will not give up on you. He will not suddenly decide that you are inconvenient or not worth his time. He has made a covenant with you that cannot be broken. He will not go back on his word under any circumstances. Mountains could crumble and fall, and the Lord your God will not overlook you.

Loving Father, I am your child, and you are my Father. Reveal the depths of your loving heart toward me as I lean into your presence. I love you.

COMPLETELY CLEARED

[Love] keeps no record of wrongs.

1 Corinthians 13:5 NIV

The definition of the love in 1 Corithians is probably one of the most quoted passages of the Bible. People are drawn to the beautiful description of true love. While it's often used in relation to other people, every aspect of that description can be superimposed onto God. God is patient, kind, and long-suffering. God does not keep a record of wrongs.

God's love, perfectly displayed by Jesus, is yours to experience. He offers it to you without hesitation or limit. When you submit your life to him, he gives you unending access to his extravagant love. As such, he does not keep a record of your wrongs. The slate has been wiped clean by the blood of Jesus. Not only does he forgive your sins, but he forgets them. Today, breathe deep in the security of God's love.

Lord, thank you for the freedom I find in your love. Thank you for your mercy when I should be paying the price for my sins. Thank you for your unending and undeserved grace.

BEYOND MEASURE

We know how much God loves us, and we have put our trust in his love. God is love, and all who live in love live in God, and God lives in them.

1 John 4:16 NLT

God is love. He doesn't muster up love or choose to love people. He *is* the embodiment of love. It's not just something he does; it's who he is. His love for you is pure, complete, and unconditional. He draws you toward him with kindness, and in his presence, he offers you everything you need.

Seek to stay in constant connection with God. Abide in his love and give him access to every part of your life. Let his love define how you act, speak, and make choices. Let his love define how you think about yourself and others. Experiencing God's love is not a one-time experience but an ongoing invitation.

God, thank you for your faithful and extravagant love. Remind me to seek after it daily. May your love impact everything I say and do.

COMING OR GOING

The LORD will protect you from all evil;
He will keep your soul.
The LORD will guard your going out and your coming in
From this time and forever.

PSALM 121:7-8 NASB

When you leave your home and when you safely return, God himself guards you. He watches over you and keeps you safe. No matter what this coming year holds, God goes with you. If you let him, he will guide you through each of your days.

Trust God to lead you. He is full of wisdom, faithfulness, and peace. He is aware of every trial, trap, and wrong turn that is ahead of you. He knows your path much better than you do. Lean on his understanding and find peace in the skill of his leadership.

Wise God, I trust you to guard me in goodness and to lead me in kindness no matter where I go. May your peace be my plentiful portion every step of my journey. Thank you.

A BRIGHT HOPE

"Look, God's dwelling is with humanity, and he will live with them. They will be his peoples, and God himself will be with them and will be their God. He will wipe away every tear from their eyes. Death will be no more; grief, crying, and pain will be no more, because the previous things have passed away."

REVELATION 21:3-4 CSB

No matter what this past year has brought you through or where this next year may take you, God is faithful to his promises. He will not leave you even for a moment. Beyond the scope of this short life lies greater hope. One day you will dwell with Christ in his kingdom. You will experience the glorious perfection you were intended for.

When you go through seasons of suffering, remember that the best is yet to come. Whatever pain you experience now can't compare to the goodness of eternity with God. In that place, death will be no more; mourning, crying, and pain will be no more. Until then, hold onto the bright and faithful hope of Jesus. He has promised to be with you until the end of the age.

My God, I believe there is so much goodness ahead. I trust you, my living and faithful hope.